Historic Tales
— *of* —
VICTORIA, TEXAS

Historic Tales
— *of* —
VICTORIA, TEXAS

TAMARA JOY DIAZ

THE
History
PRESS

Published by The History Press
Charleston, SC
www.historypress.com

All images are from the author's collection unless otherwise noted.

First published 2024

Manufactured in the United States

ISBN 9781467158695

Library of Congress Control Number: 2024941836

Notice: The information in this book is true and complete to the best of our knowledge. It is offered without guarantee on the part of the author or The History Press. The author and The History Press disclaim all liability in connection with the use of this book.

Dedicated in loving memory to my mother,
Sharon Lee Gratton Hanson

CONTENTS

ACKNOWLEDGEMENTS

This book would not have been possible, first and foremost, without the excellent research assistance provided by Kevin Oliver and Brittany Rodriguez at the Victoria Regional History Center, located at the University of Houston–Victoria. The history center is an invaluable history repository for Crossroads communities.

I am indebted to the historians who wrote before me, particularly Henry Wolff Jr., Ana Carolina Castillo Crimm, members of Victoria Preservation, Inc. and the Texas Historical Commission, Victor Marion Rose, John Joseph Linn and many others.

The idea for this book was sparked and fostered by Keith Kohn, former executive editor of the *Victoria Advocate*. *Advocate* editors Becky Cooper and Jon Wilcox also edited some of the copy early in the process. The three have been invaluable mentors. I owe much to the Victoria newspaper and its staff.

Finally, Blanche de Leon, a descendant of Victoria's founders, has been a friend and mentor to me and has generously shared her family's story. Her steadfastness in reclaiming her family's place in history has been an inspiration to me.

INTRODUCTION

Stephen Fuller Austin is called the father of Texas, but did you know there was another? In the time of Austin's colony, Empresario Don Martin de Leon founded Victoria southwest of Austin's. Austin and De Leon were the only successful Mexican empresarios in Texas history. While Austin triumphed as the ultimate founder of the state, the De Leon family, being of Mexican and Spanish descent, was vilified after the Texas Revolution and temporarily exiled from the new republic. This, despite having aided the revolution with money, livestock and weapons. Some members of the family even rode with revolution hero Juan Seguín.

This book tells the story of the founding of Victoria, the De Leon family, their tragic exile and eventual return, as well as the stories of other figures in Victoria's two-hundred-year history, right up to a modern businesswoman running a historic real estate agency near the heart of the city.

Chapter 1

VICTORIA'S FOUNDER, EMPRESARIO DON MARTIN DE LEON

De Leon Plaza has been refurbished, the statues of our founders bolted in place and De Leon descendants in the hundreds gathered in Victoria, from all directions on the map. Speeches made. Dances spun at the Bicentennial Ball. Honorary Mass attended and historic homes toured.

And it all comes back to one man's decision to bring his family, and forty-one others, north from Mexico to the banks of the Guadalupe River two hundred years ago.

TWO HUNDRED YEARS AGO

On April 13, 1824, Martin de Leon was granted permission to establish a colony with the small town of Nuestra Señora de Guadalupe de Jesus near a fordable passage through the Guadalupe River. The river had been discovered and named by Martin's great-grandfather more than 150 years earlier.

That year, 1824, was also when the Marquis de Lafayette, the famed General Lafayette of the American Revolution, returned to the United States for a grand tour, and Noah Cushing of Quebec patented the washing machine—albeit a primitive model. The first section of New York City's Fifth Avenue was laid, and a Harrisburg, Pennsylvania newspaper published the results of the first public opinion poll conducted in the United States.

Also in 1824, Guadalupe Victoria, a friend to the fledgling town, took office as the first president of the United Mexican States.

As Nuestra Señora de Guadalupe de Jesus, now called Victoria in honor of the first Mexican president, celebrates its bicentennial, it is fitting to trace the city's founding story—the story of the De Leon family, the originators who lived, ranched, worshipped, loved, adjudicated and multiplied in and around the colony they created.

BEGINNINGS

Martin de Leon was born in 1765 to Bernardo de Leon and Maria Galvan. A Franciscan tutor educated Martin where his family lived in Cruillas, Nuevo Santander, New Spain, just south of modern-day Texas.

On hand at the Victoria Regional History Center is a copy of Ana Carolina Castillo Crimm's *De Leon: A Tejano Family History*, a superb source for information about the De Leon family. The history center also has a plethora of other historical materials related to the founding of Victoria.

"Martin's family, proud of their light skin and Spanish heritage, disdained the dark, single-room adobe homes of the Indians," Crimm wrote. "In his own eyes, he felt his family was as good as anyone born in Spain. To the newly arrived Spaniards, however, Martin and his family were second-class citizens, untrustworthy criollos."

The De Leons were Spanish but born in the Americas. Martin's father, Bernardo, was a pioneer, modeling the adventurous spirit for his son. He was among 2,500 other colonists who went north to settle Nuevo Santander, Crimm wrote.

He originally settled in Burgos, "the westernmost of the settlements in the foothills of the Sierra Madres," Crimm noted. Sometime after 1749, he married Maria Galvan.

By the 1760s, investors in the northern colony had "discovered veins of silver, copper, gold, zinc and lead in the mountains around the towns." Settlers soon moved to the mining towns.

"Within a year, the population at San Carlos and Cruillas jumped to 15,000," Crimm wrote. "Among those requesting permission to move to Cruillas was Bernardo De Leon, with his wife, Maria Galvan, and one-year-old Martin." Bernardo gained wealth from Cruillas, Crimm added.

Importantly to the story of Victoria, Bernardo instructed his children that "just because they had not been among the elite class did not mean that avenues of opportunity were closed to them, especially not on the northern frontier of New Spain," Crimm wrote.

When Martin was grown, he became a mayordomo, the owner and leader of a mule train. These trains were the only way to get supplies into the northern reaches. "Martin de Leon, as a mayordomo, hired his own staff of assistants, consisting of between three and ten or more men," Crimm wrote. "During his five years in the profession, from 1785 to 1790, Martin de Leon concentrated on the lucrative mining trade."

It was during this time, Crimm added, that he may have become familiar with "the lands north of the Rio Bravo del Norte [later, the Rio Grande]."

At the age of twenty-five, De Leon enlisted in the Spanish army in New Spain. Since he was not born in Spain, he could advance only to the rank of captain, which he did. "He could still gain social distinction, some political influence, and an extensive *fuero*, or military legal right," Crimm wrote. "Martin could be assured of a pension and a land grant."

He also "caught the eye of his commander's daughter, Patricia de la Garza," Crimm wrote. She had a sizable dowry, and he had earned a land grant as a reward for his service. "The young couple, looking hopefully across the river and into the new century, were part of the slow but steady, ongoing Spanish expansion northward," Crimm wrote.

The couple had two ranches, at two separate times, in Texas, one on the Nueces River and one on the Aransas. Their ten children—Fernando, Maria Candelaria, Jose Silvestre, Maria Guadalupe, Jose Felix, Agapito, Maria de Jesus, Refugia, Augustina and Francisca—were born between 1798 and 1818. Blanche de Leon, a sixth-generation descendant of the founders, claims both Felix and Augustina among her forebears. The De Leon sons owned land surrounding Victoria. The women married well and became influential figures in both Victoria and Goliad history.

Unsettled Spanish and Mexican politics and rebellions interfered with both De Leon ranching ventures. Around 1812, the family went back to Burgos and Soto la Marina—home of Patricia's family—and to the relative safety of the settled region.

From here, Martin de Leon would apply for an empresarial contract to settle a colony on the Guadalupe River, Crimm wrote.

"They were resolute in their relationships and mission. Architecturally building on the past, they envisioned the future and beyond," Blanche de Leon said of Martin and Patricia and the family.

GUADALUPE RIVER: SITE CHOSEN FOR COLONY, GUADALUPE VICTORIA

It begins with the river.

Victoria's founder chose the location of the town, two hundred years ago, simply because the Guadalupe River was close by and fordable near town.

The Guadalupe River historical marker on South Moody Street reads, in its first sentence, "Discovered in this vicinity on April 14, 1689, by Alonso de Leon." Alonso de Leon was Martin de Leon's great-grandfather.

All the land over which the river flows belonged to Spain and was called New Spain at the time of the Spanish discovery and naming of the Guadalupe River in 1689. Native peoples had lived along the river's banks for tens of thousands of years at the time of its discovery by Spain.

When news reached Spanish officials, in the mid-1680s, that the French had founded a colony on the northern Gulf Coast, they sent Alonso de Leon to "find the foreign interlopers and extirpate their colony," according to a Texas State Historical Association (TSHA) article.

De Leon would lead four expeditions north of the Rio Grande in southeast Texas. His first two expeditions found no evidence of French colonists; however, he was sent on a third expedition, launched in May 1688, "in response to news that a White man dwelled among Indians in a rancheria (temporary settlement) to the North of the Rio Grande," according to the TSHA.

City sign near downtown and the original town site.

De Leon's fourth expedition discovered the ruins of Fort St. Louis near present-day Victoria and named the Guadalupe River in honor of Our Lady of Guadalupe, all during the month of April 1689.

Moving forward in time to another April day, this one in 1824, and the final two sentences of the historic marker: "Here, at a ford, used since Indian days, Empresario Martin de Leon founded the town of Victoria in 1824."

"On April 8, 1824, [Martin] de Leon...respectfully petitioned for permission to found a colony on the Guadalupe River in Texas," Crimm wrote. "De Leon promised, as empresario, to bring 41 families from Nuevo Santander at his own expense to establish the town of Villa de Nuestra Senora de Guadalupe de Jesus [later named Victoria Guadalupe and then simply Victoria]."

Thus, Victoria was born of a passable spot—a ford—in the Guadalupe River.

THE DE LEON FAMILY'S TRAIL TO VICTORIA

Fourteen-year-old Maria Candelaria planned to marry her childhood companion after she turned fifteen. Her 1818 marriage would join two influential ranching families in New Spain, the Aldrete and De Leon families.

The De Leon family traveled from Soto la Marina (in present-day Mexico) to southeastern Texas, where the young bridegroom, seventeen-year-old Jose Miguel Aldrete, waited with his family near present-day Victoria. "The choice of bridegroom was no surprise," wrote Crimm. "Seventeen-year-old Jose Miguel Aldrete had grown up with Candelaria, and the two had known each other for most of their lives."

This journey into Texas was the family's second attempt to establish themselves here, and the size of the family was growing. Martin and Patricia de Leon soon celebrated the birth of their tenth child, a daughter. Martin de Leon wanted to ensure he would have enough land for his children as they grew into adulthood and started families of their own. He grew concerned as he watched Anglo-Americans colonize the land around him and decided to seek a colonization grant himself before nothing was left, Crimm wrote.

Mexico won independence from Spain in 1821, and De Leon and most of his family returned to Soto la Marina to recruit colonists. He had to have a sizable number of willing colonists before his grant would be approved.

Meanwhile, some Mexican officials grew uneasy because "Texas had always excited the envy of the United States and colonization would afford

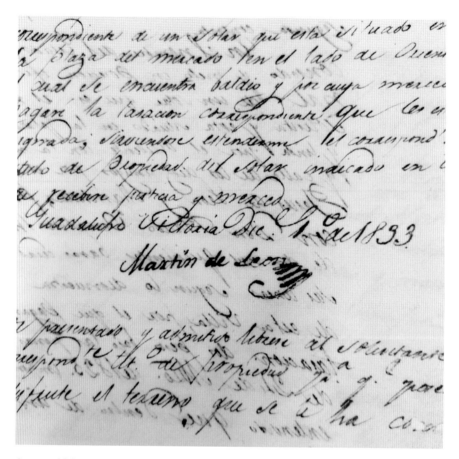

A copy of Martin de Leon's signature from the De Leon box collection at the Victoria Regional History Center.

the United States the easiest and most advantageous method to obtain it," Crimm noted in her book.

De Leon managed to recruit forty-one families, and his colonization grant was approved on April 13, 1824, according to the TSHA. He became an empresario and founded Victoria with that grant, the "only predominantly Mexican colony in Texas."

"Driven by and delivering every bit of what they [Martin and Patricia de Leon] promised, they were successful because of the love and respect they had for one another and others, for the land and its creatures," Blanche de Leon said. "With their wits and each other, they raised this community out of the wilderness that it once was not too long ago. And often, they thanked God for His blessings and asked for His continued guidance."

"Martin's main purpose—providing lands for his sons and daughters—would be accomplished," Crimm wrote.

On Bridge Street, next to the Victoria Police Department, a historical marker designates the home of Empresario Martin de Leon. As previously reported in the *Advocate*, the author of an undated article in the De Leon collection at the Victoria Regional History Center wrote that the first home of Martin and Patricia de Leon was on "'the present-day site of St. Mary's Church.' The home consisted of 'one large room, a 10-foot hallway and a small room.'"

While the family had this home in town, they also had a 22,140-acre ranch in southeastern Victoria County.

"De Leon stood six feet tall and was skilled as a horseman and Indian fighter; Indians called him 'Capitan Vacas Muchas' ('Captain Plenty of Cows') since he often placated raiding parties by feeding them beef," according to the TSHA.

Even though the family had large tracts of land outside of town, most of what remains today to mark the De Leons' founding legacy is in downtown Victoria. For example, Patrica de Leon donated the land St. Mary's Catholic Church sits on upon her death.

Most of the De Leon ranch land and other De Leon properties and belongings were taken from the family when they were exiled shortly after the Texas Revolution, even though they supported and assisted the revolutionaries. "The bitter aftermath of the Texas Revolution was felt most directly by the Mexican settlements along the Guadalupe and San Antonio Rivers, those closest to the Anglo-American colonies of Austin and DeWitt," David Montejano wrote in *Anglos and Mexicans in the Making of Texas, 1836–1986*. "Here the Mexican communities were subjugated and in many cases expelled."

Martin de Leon died years before the expulsion. The revolution scattered his children, but Patricia de Leon and her remaining children were forced to leave Victoria with few belongings.

As Martin Dryer put it in a 1972 *Houston Chronicle* article in the De Leon Collection at the history center, "They were persecuted, murdered, robbed of their land and properties and driven into exile."

DOÑA PATRICIA DE LEON: HONORING OUR FOUNDING MOTHER

She fell in love with a dashing young captain in her father's command, married him and helped finance their move to a frontier "drenched in blood." She brought "religion, schools, and an enriched social and cultural life to South Texas," a land once thought uninhabitable, historian Teresa Paloma Acosta wrote.

Doña Patricia de Leon was among the first Texans, a Tejana, a wife, a mother and a pioneer. She was many things throughout the course of her life: a devoted mother and grandmother, a patriot, an outcast, once one of the wealthiest women in the state, at another time stripped of her possessions. She held sway over her four sons, as all Tejana mothers did, urging them not to possess firearms at a time when Texas was wrapped in a vicious uncertainty that saw military excursions of unusual cruelty.

She was nearing fifty years old when she and Martin founded Victoria. He was in his sixties. Patricia bore ten children within twenty years and had four sons, six sons-in-law and more than twenty grandchildren.

"The Tejana women like Doña Patricia made their own decisions and played an important role in family matters. Women may have remained subservient to their husbands, but they were never subservient to their sons, nephews, or grandsons," Crimm wrote. "Spanish and Mexican cultures gave their women the right to demand respect, obedience, and power within the family."

Years earlier, in 1795, thirty-three-year-old Martin had married twenty-year-old Patricia de la Garza of Soto la Marina. She was "born about 1775 on the east coast of Mexico not far from present-day Brownsville," Acosta wrote in *Las Tejanas: 300 Years of History*, on hand at the Victoria Regional History Center. She was born into a wealthy family, but "on the frontier, the number of appropriate suitors was slim for someone of the landed aristocracy such as the de la Garza family."

"[Martin] was not wealthy, but he was hardworking, and with the potential for a successful military career, he was still a promising prospect for the twenty-year-old Patricia," Crimm wrote. "With the family's approval, the self-confident and dynamic captain courted and won her hand."

From her father, Patricia received forty-nine animals to start a ranch, a common dowry on the frontier. But from her godfather, Don Angel Perez of Soto la Marina, she received 9,800 pesos, a rich sum. The money would always be legally hers, "although Martin could administer the dowry and invest it for profit," Crimm wrote.

A forensic portrait of Patricia de Leon by Lois Gibson of Houston, commissioned by the De Leon family for the bicentennial. *Blanche de Leon*.

On January 1, 1801, Patricia and Martin went before a notary public at Presas del Rey in the Eastern Interior Provinces of New Spain, where she "signed over her dowry of almost 10,000 pesos in cash, goods, and livestock to her husband," Crimm noted.

The couple was investing everything to establish a ranch on the Texas frontier. They would have two at two separate times, one on the Nueces River and one on the Aransas, before applying for and receiving an empresario grant to found Victoria. During that time, Mexico changed hands several times.

In 1821, Mexico gained independence from Spain, but the Mexican government teetered as many newborn governments do. It eventually fell into the hands of a dictator: the self-styled "Napoleon of the West," General Antonio Lopez de Santa Anna.

But many years before Santa Anna, there was blood on the Texas frontier, once delivered in 1813 by a Barcelona-born general named José Joaquin de Arredondo y Mioño, historians Bryan Burrough, Chris Tomlinson and Jason Stanford wrote.

"Arredondo was renowned in Mexico for killing every prisoner he took, no matter the number, no matter the conditions," they wrote. And he went on a killing spree in Texas, trying to put down uprisings for Mexican independence. Texas Mexicans fled, but he killed everyone he caught.

And riding with Arredondo, perhaps taking notes, was a young officer named Santa Anna.

This cauldron of revolution, counterrevolution and bloodshed was the setting for Doña Patricia de Leon's family rearing. But she and Martin persisted, returning to Mexico when the family's safety demanded it. This may be why Patricia insisted in later years that her sons not possess firearms. She had reason to disdain them.

In a period of brief stability within the nascent Mexican government, Martin applied for and was granted a colonial contract to found Victoria, which he named Nuestra Señora de Guadalupe Victoria. Patricia became the founding Mother of Texas.

"Before it all fell apart in 1835, more than thirty empresarios attempted to bring settlers to Texas," Stephen Harrington wrote in *Big Wonderful Thing: A History of Texas*, a University of Texas Press publication.

Among those who succeeded was Martin de Leon. De Leon, who was just approaching his sixties, was one of the most renowned figures north of the Rio Grande when he filed for empresario status. The son of aristocratic peninsulares [pureblood Spaniards who were born in Spain but

Detail of the clay statue of Martin and Patricia de Leon by Laredo artist Armando Hinojosa. The statue was cast in bronze for the bicentennial.

had moved to live in the Spanish colonies], *he and his equally industrious wife, Patricia, had staked out a future in Texas.*

Patricia immediately established a church and school in the fledgling colony, overseeing the educational and spiritual needs of the frontier families.

Martin died of cholera before the Texas Revolution, leaving Patricia and her sons to decide a course of action. They supported the Texians, smuggling goods to support the Texian army and fighting alongside them in the bid for independence from Mexico. It would cost her everything.

When Martin died, he left Patricia a wealthy widow, if not the wealthiest woman in Texas; however, prejudicial feeling against anyone of Mexican origin after Texas gained its independence would see her stripped of most of her belongings and exiled, with her family. She fought for and gained much of her land back, dying in 1850, still embroiled in lawsuits that her children would assume after her death.

In her will, she left her homestead, at the corner of Main and Church Streets, to the Catholic Church.

JUAN LINN: A GOOD AND FAITHFUL FRIEND AND CO-FOUNDER

John J. Linn, a faithful friend to the De Leon family, helped Doña Patricia de Leon flee Texas when the remnants of the founding family were exiled for several years, Crimm said in a video for the TSHA. John was lovingly called "Juan" by the Mexican colonists in Victoria.

Martin de Leon "needed additional colonists" to meet his contractual obligation as an empresario, Crimm wrote. "Among the later arrivals were the Carbajal family and the four Benavides brothers," Crimm noted. "De Leon also found sixteen Anglo-American families who had already moved into the area illegally, including John Linn, John D. Wright, and Joseph Ware."

De Leon accepted these men, Crimm wrote, making the Victoria colony remarkably inclusive. One Mexican official who visited the colony in 1828 "indicated that there were individuals in the Victoria colony from Canada, the United States, Ireland, France, and Germany. Unlike Austin's settlements on the Colorado, Martin de Leon's colony was, by necessity, multicultural from its inception," Crimm wrote. The Mexican authorities did not all "approve of the varied ethnic flavor of the Victoria colony," Crimm noted.

Linn was one of those varied flavors, but at heart he was, more than anything else, a Texian. He appreciated the beauty of his adopted homeland. He remained faithful to the De Leon family throughout their exile, writing to them frequently to keep them informed. He and his brother Edward assumed legal battles on behalf of the family.

In later years, Linn was a good friend and mentor to Victor Rose, the storied one-time editor of the *Victoria Advocate* and early chronicler of the city.

MARTIN'S DEATH AND THE ASCENDANCE AND TROUBLES OF HIS SONS

Ten years after he founded Victoria, on July 18, 1834, Martin de Leon died of cholera at the age of seventy. Two of the empresario's four sons, also considered founders of Victoria, were murdered within a decade after his death.

Two cholera epidemics swept through South Texas, one in the summer of 1833 and another in the summer of 1834, Crimm noted. San Antonio and Goliad were the two largest towns in South Texas at the time. Victoria was home to only about three hundred people. "Ninety-one of Goliad's less than 1,000 residents died" in the cholera epidemic that claimed De Leon's life, Crimm wrote.

Historical markers at Evergreen Cemetery within the Historical Grave Shrine of the De Leon Family honor all four of Martin and Patricia de Leon's sons. Fernando, Silvestre, Felix and Agapito de Leon helped their father found and govern the Guadalupe Victoria Colony.

FERNANDO DE LEON

Fernando was the eldest of the De Leons' ten children, born in 1798. He was land commissioner for the colony. He was widowed young, in 1825, and eventually remarried. Fernando was the only one of the four De Leon sons to live past the age of fifty. When his younger brother Silvestre was murdered, Fernando adopted his children.

SILVESTRE DE LEON

Silvestre de Leon was the empresario's third child, born in 1802. He served as both an alcalde (mayor) and a judge in Victoria.

He was once "called on to rule on a case involving his own father," Crimm wrote. "Don Martin was accused of shooting a hog belonging to a Mexican resident of Victoria." Silvestre asked his father if the allegations were true. He said that he did shoot the hog but only after it destroyed his garden.

Silvestre asked his father if he had a "lawful fence" to keep hogs out of his garden, to which his father replied that "it was not the best," John Linn wrote in *Fifty Years in Texas*.

But then Don Martin asked his son if he would rule against his own father. "Don Silvestre replied that in his capacity as a public officer the ties that bound him as an individual were inoperative. On the bench he would perform his duty with strict impartiality, but off the bench he became again the dutiful son," Linn wrote.

Silvestre ordered his father to pay restitution of twenty dollars. "Don Martin promptly paid the amount, with the remark that he was proud of such a son, to the disappointment of a crowd that had collected to see some fun," Linn recorded.

Silvestre supported the Texian army during the Texas Revolution, supplying the troops with provisions, livestock and military equipment, Craig H. Roell wrote in a Texas State Historical Association article.

He also served in the Texas army and "upon the occupation of Guadalupe Victoria by Gen. Jose de Urrea, [Silvestre] De Leon was arrested by the Mexican Army as a traitor," Roell noted.

Despite his fidelity to Texas independence, he suffered a cruel fate. After the victory at San Jacinto, Silvestre "fell victim to the severe prejudice directed against all Texans of Mexican descent." He was exiled to Louisiana with other members of his family and lost "his land, livestock, and most possessions to fortune hunters," Roell continued.

He returned to Victoria County and tried to use the legal system to regain his lands, but while returning from a trip to Louisiana, "he was ambushed, murdered and robbed in 1842 under still mysterious circumstances."

Crimm noted in her book that Silvestre's land was located where present-day Nursery is situated.

FELIX DE LEON

Felix was born in 1806. He lived until 1850, around one year longer than his mother, Patricia.

When Felix was about fourteen or fifteen years old, he accompanied his father on a trip to procure the shipping services of a band of pirates. "A pirate named Ramon Le Fou had agreed to ship de Leon's goods in exchange for a pardon from Spanish officials. De Leon agreed to contact government officials," Crimm wrote. "Le Fou and his men had offered transportation, and when de Leon came aboard with his son, Felix, they had insured de Leon's success by holding Felix as insurance."

De Leon got pardon papers for the pirates, who then returned Felix to him.

Felix died in 1850, without warning, Crimm wrote.

AGAPITO DE LEON

Agapito was the youngest of the De Leons' four sons. Born in 1808, he was a teenager when his father founded Victoria. Even so, he is considered a founder of the town, as noted on his historic marker in Evergreen Cemetery.

Crimm wrote in her book that Agapito died in the 1833 cholera epidemic, but the historic marker notes that, rather, he "was assassinated by Mabry 'Mustang' Gray, leader of a gang systematically robbing Texans of Mexican descent, after the close of the War for Independence." The Texas Historical Commission also states that Agapito was murdered by Gray.

Agapito and two ranch hands caught Gray rustling their cattle, A.B.J. Hammett wrote in his book *Empresario: Don Martin de Leon*. Agapito pointed out the De Leon brand, and after heated words were exchanged, Gray killed Agapito.

Gray was never brought to justice, Hammett noted, and is "enshrined and recorded as one of the Texas heroes on the San Jacinto Monument."

Agapito was twenty-eight years old when he was murdered. "Agapito was found floating in the Guadalupe," De Leon descendant Blanche de Leon said.

DON RAFAEL ANTONIO MANCHOLA: DE LEON POLITICAL ALLY, FRIEND AND SON-IN-LAW

Martin and Patricia de Leon had ten children, born within a twenty-year span between 1798 and 1818. The couple had four sons (Fernando, Jose Silvestre, Jose Felix and Agapito) and six daughters (Maria Candelaria, Maria Guadalupe, Maria de Jesus, Refugia, Augustina and Francisca).

The youngest daughter, Francisca, by Spanish tradition, took care of her aging mother. After Patricia died, she married Vincente Dosal in Victoria in 1849 and had children of her own.

In 1825, Maria Guadalupe married Desiderio Garcia, one of the colonists in Victoria Guadalupe, but the couple never had children. "Maria Guadalupe married a second time to Cesario de la Garza," Blanche de Leon said. The union produced many descendants.

In 1831, Augustina married Placido Benavides, and in 1832, Refugia married Jose Maria Jesus Carbajal.

The eldest daughter, Maria Candelaria, married Jose Miquel Aldrete in 1818.

Daughter Maria de Jesus married Rafael Antonio Manchola in 1824, the year of Victoria's founding. Maria de Jesus was fourteen years old when she was betrothed to twenty-four-year-old Manchola. "It was an excellent match for Maria de Jesus, but it was even better for promoting Don Martin's political connections, since the Manchola family were influential at La Bahia [Goliad]," Crimm wrote in *De Leon: A Tejano Family History*.

At Goliad, the government consisted of a mayor and town council. De Leon's sons-in-law Aldrete and Manchola had influence they used in favor of De Leon, Crimm noted. In Goliad, on the courthouse square, a marker designates the contributions of Manchola as an "early Goliad leader." He "was born to a Spanish aristocratic family circa 1800. In 1822 arrived in La Bahia," the marker reads, in part, and he "became a state deputy in the Coahuila and Texas Legislature [Mexico]. He also served as alcalde in Goliad."

Important to Victoria's formation, "during the 1829 legislative session, Manchola helped establish the municipality of Guadalupe Victoria." This gave De Leon more control over the fledgling town, allowing for legal control from within, rather than having to rely on all adjudications from nearby La Bahia (Goliad).

Manchola served his father-in-law as his "attorney and agent in legal matters and official correspondence," according to an article in *The History and Heritage of Victoria County* at the regional history center. "Manchola was considered one of the key persons involved in the establishment of the new community and thus was included in the list of the ten friends," according to the article.

Historian A.B.J. Hammett wrote it was Manchola who petitioned the legislature to have the name "La Bahia" changed to "Goliad." "He explained that the name of La Bahia del Espiritu Santo had little meaning but that the name of Goliad, an anagram from the important letters in the surname Hidalgo, the heroic giant of the Revolution had great meaning," Hammett wrote in *The Empresario Don Martin de Leon*, also on hand at the history center.

Miguel Hidalgo y Costilla was a Catholic priest who called the common people of Mexico to revolt at the outset of the Mexican War of Independence. The war began in 1810 and lasted until Mexico gained independence from Spain in 1821; however, Hidalgo was killed by a firing squad in 1811, raising him to martyrdom and making him a powerful symbol in Mexico's fight.

"Hidalgo was a priest with a pistol in his cassock," T.R. Fehrenbach wrote in *Fire & Blood: A History of Mexico*.

Hidalgo was a hero to Manchola and the people of La Bahia. Manchola served in a military capacity at one point.

"In the year 1831, Rafael Manchola commanded the troops at the Presidio La Bahia," Hammett wrote. "Like the other members of the De Leon family, Rafael Manchola acquired large tracts of land and established himself in the cattle business. His famous brand was one of the first registered in Don Martin de Leon's capital city of Guadalupe Victoria in the year 1838."

Manchola died in 1833, however, leaving Maria de Jesus the land.

"She became one of the large landowners around Guadalupe Victoria by reason of her husband's services to the Republic of Mexico," Roy Grimes wrote in *300 Years in Victoria County*.

"As wife, she would become a huge landowner in Goliad," Blanche de Leon noted on January 12, 2024. "Madame Manchola received lands as did Patricia after both their husbands were dead. Rare for women to have received, but they were Spanish, and unlike Anglo women, had that right."

Maria de Jesus had one child with Rafael, a daughter named Francisca who married D. Cristobal Morales in Soto la Marina, in 1846, Blanche de Leon noted on January 25, 2024.

When Patricia de Leon died, she left cattle and mortgages she owned in Louisiana to Maria de Jesus. She also left her "title to one of the two building lots in Victoria on which she held income-producing mortgages," Crimm noted.

SONS-IN-LAW:
PLACIDO BENAVIDES AND JOSE CARBAJAL

Augustina de Leon married Placido Benavides in 1831. Benavides played a significant role in both the establishment of the Victoria colony, as he was twice alcalde, and in Texas's bid for independence, riding with Tejano volunteers in Stephen F. Austin's army in late 1835, as the fighting began.

"The only bright spots in Austin's command were the 135 Tejano volunteers led by Placido Benavides from Victoria and Juan Seguín from San Antonio," Crimm wrote. "They did not question authority, debate his orders, or vote on his commands. They remained loyal, trustworthy, and obedient."

While alcalde, or mayor, Benavides even had the courage to stand up to a Mexican general who demanded the body of another Texas patriot, his brother-in-law Jose Maria Jesus Carbajal. That loyalty and bravery would be repaid with expulsion for Benavides and his family simply because of their Mexican origin. He would later die of yellow fever while in exile.

At 301 South Main Street, a historic marker denotes where Benavides built his home in Victoria—the Round Top House, called the Citadel of Victoria. The Round Top House was a touch of Spanish style built by Benavides, who came to Guadalupe Victoria in 1828 from Tamaulipas. He was twenty-two years old at the time.

"He began construction of what would later be called Placido's Round House. The building was in fact a Spanish-style torreon, the circular, tower-like, defensive turret, with toneras or gun slits on the lower floors, a style which the Spanish had learned from the Moors," Crimm noted. The Spanish had been using this style of dwelling for many years on the frontier to defend against Indian attacks.

The historic marker notes, "The house served as a place of refuge for the citizens of Victoria during the Comanche raid of 1840," some two years after its builder perished during his banishment.

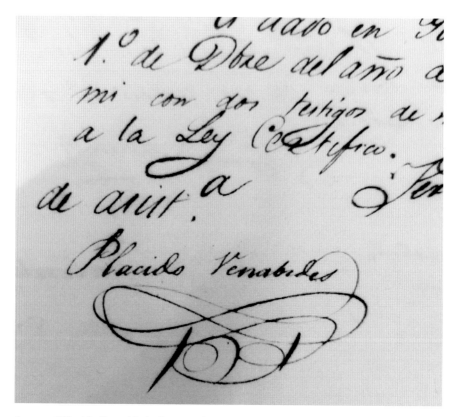

A copy of Placido Benavides's signature from the De Leon box collection at the Victoria Regional History Center.

"Benavides' military and political acumen were most beneficial to the budding colony," David Urbano wrote in *The Saga of a Revolutionary Family: The Martin de Leon Family of Texas,* on hand at the Victoria Regional History Center.

"In 1832 and again in 1834 he was elected alcalde. In other capacities he organized militia expeditions against marauding Indians and offered his Round Top House as a refuge for many colonists during attacks," Urbano added.

Benavides built the Round Top House and married eighteen-year-old Augustina de Leon in late 1832, Crimm wrote. At the same time, Refugia de Leon married Jose Maria Jesus Carbajal.

"The match between Placido Benavides and Augustina was more to Doña Patricia's liking," Crimm wrote. "Placido was hardworking, determined to succeed, and, above all, Catholic."

Carbajal was a Protestant, which bothered Doña Patricia, a devoted Catholic. But it would not be long before the De Leon brothers and brothers-in-law would become a "tight-knit group," Crimm added. Carbajal would be hunted by the Mexican army for treason, having served in the Monclova congress in the rebellious Coahuila y Texas state government in March 1835—the first blushes of revolution in Texas.

The state government wanted to adhere to the Mexican constitution of 1824, while Antonio de Lopez de Santa Anna pulled all power to himself in a centralist government—a dictatorship.

General Ugartechea and a detail of mounted Mexican soldiers followed Carbajal back to Victoria, with orders to arrest him. Alcalde Don Placido Benavides and a few dozen armed Victoria citizens stood their ground.

As Juan Linn recounted in his *Reminiscences of Fifty Years in Texas*, an officer representing "Colonel Ugartechea [demanded] the body of Carbajal. Placido Benavides returned the order and said to the officer that he could inform Colonel Ugartechea that neither the body of Carbajal nor the body of any other citizen of Victoria would be delivered into the hands of the military. By this time, the troops were completely surrounded by armed citizens."

The Mexican soldados left without Carbajal, who was hidden away on Doña Patricia's ranch.

By mid-June 1836, a couple of months after Texas won its independence at San Jacinto, Anglo Texans in and around Victoria were worried about the possible return of Mexican troops and saw even their Tejano allies as a threat. Doña Patricia de Leon protested her rude treatment at the hands of Texian soldiers to authorities, but to no avail, Crimm wrote.

The De Leon family was forced out of the colony they had founded. They packed up what belongings they could and loaded mule-drawn wagons and carts. "From the ranches to the south came Placido, a pregnant Augustina, and their two girls," Crimm wrote. As the family gathered to make their exit, "in the bustle and confusion, the Anglos crowded around rudely to jeer, reaching out to snatch jewelry from the women."

The family went to New Orleans aboard a ship, via Indianola, and were kept informed of goings-on in Texas by their ever-faithful friend Juan Linn. By 1838, Patricia de Leon and some family members were sojourning on Benavides family land in Opelousas, Louisiana.

"Worn out from his exertions, Placido came down with the dreaded disease [yellow fever]. There was no medical help, and the family was devastated when he died that summer," Crimm wrote. "The family buried

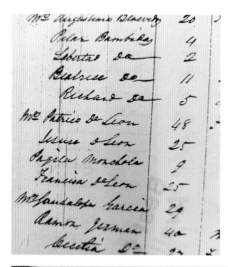

Left: Patricia de Leon and others listed on a ship's manifest from Indianola to New Orleans, after the exile.

Below: Certified copy of the ship's manifest from the exile of the De Leon family, on hand at the Victoria Regional History Center.

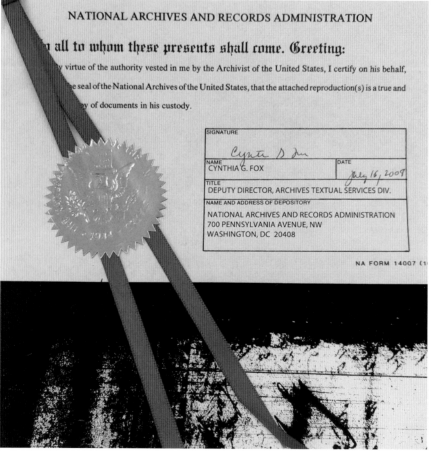

him beside little Crecencia [Carbajal, his niece] in the Benavides family plot. The following year, death struck again. Sylvestre's wife, Rosalia, succumbed. She, too, was laid to rest in the cemetery at Opelousas, Louisiana, far from their Texas home."

On a final note, Texas Revolution historian Stephen Hardin noted that the popular observation that first-generation Texas Rangers could "shoot like a Tennessean, ride like a Mexican and fight like the Devil" was only possible because "comrades such as Juan Seguín and Placido Benavides proved excellent instructors."

IMPORTANT FIGURES IN THE TEXAS REVOLUTION

In October 1835, Sylvestre de Leon and his brother-in-law Placido Benavides rode with about thirty vaqueros and a contingent of Texas rebels toward Goliad's Presidio la Bahia. Theirs was the first expedition against the Mexican-held fortress in Texas's war for independence.

Among the vaqueros was another De Leon relation, Mariano Carbajal, brother of Jose Maria Carbajal. Jose Maria married Martin and Patricia de Leon's eighth child, Refugia, in 1832. So invested in Texas independence was Jose Maria Carbajal that he had to hide from the advancing Mexican armies, who would have killed him on sight for treason, Crimm wrote.

Goliad is rich in historic markers and a key stop on the Texas Independence Trail.

Among those killed in the Goliad massacre was Mariano Carbajal, Crimm noted. His name is etched into the Fannin Monument, misspelled as "Mariano Carabajal." With Colonel James Walker Fannin Jr., under the monument near the Presidio la Bahia, lie the remains of hundreds of Texian patriots, including Mariano Carbajal. The remains were discovered and buried by Texian troops after Santa Anna's surrender at San Jacinto in April 1836.

MODERN SPOKESPERSON FOR THE DE LEON FAMILY: A FEW OF BLANCHE DE LEON'S THOUGHTS

Blanche de Leon is descended from two of Martin and Patricia's children and has become a leading source and advocate of the De Leon family history.

"I am really, really in awe of Patricia," De Leon said in a lecture she presented in October 2023. "She had ten children in the midst of all this traveling. She was no slouch."

De Leon mentioned Patricia's key involvement in the formation of St. Mary's Catholic Church, noting that the church still has "one gold vessel" brought to the new colony by Patricia.

De Leon said it is her personal mission to share her family's history. "There was a history before Stephen F. Austin and James Bowie. We have stories to tell, and we should be telling them," she said.

She added to this vein in January 2024, saying, "Only Austin sits with De Leon as a successful empresarial contract during Texas's colonial period, Austin's

Martin de Leon's grandson Francisco Sylvester de Leon, date unknown. *Blanche de Leon.*

grant occurring first, then De Leon's. One is left to question why we love to celebrate Austin's 300 and not mention the work of De Leon at all. History is not meant to pick and choose what should be remembered, what should be taught."

Or, as she said in a June 2022 lecture at a meeting of the Victoria County Historical Commission, "There is no shame in embracing the Hispanic history that is unique to Victoria. It is real, and it should be honored."

Chapter 2

TWO PIONEERS WHO CAME BEFORE THE DE LEON FAMILY

In a lecture she gave at the Victoria Public Library in February 2024, Blanche de Leon told an audience of about sixty that the bicentennial is an occasion to celebrate all Victorians who have shaped the city over the years.

She named Margaret Wright and John Joseph Linn as co-founders who predated and then collaborated with her forebears Martin and Patricia de Leon. "The bicentennial is not an occasion to celebrate only Martin and Patricia but to celebrate all of us now and all of the people of Victoria from the past two hundred years," De Leon said.

Certainly, Linn was a great friend to the De Leon family and helped shape the colony, and Margaret Wright—who was established in the Victoria area at least two years before Martin de Leon came north—was called the "Little Mother of Texas" by none other than the great hero of the Texas Revolution, Sam Houston. Houston called her such because she is credited with saving several survivors of the Goliad Massacre on her Lower Mission Valley ranch on the banks of the Guadalupe River. Apparently, she even hid some of the wounded Texas soldiers under her wide skirt.

Back in 1984, Henry Wolff Jr. told the story, noting that Robert D. King of San Antonio descended from one of those men who hid in Wright's skirt. "King said the story told in his family was that Margaret helped get some of the wounded soldiers out of Mexican reach in a rather ingenious way. She wore a big skirt, and she hid them under that," Wolff wrote.

MARGARET WRIGHT

Widowed twice in Louisiana, with five children to support, Wright came west to the Lower Mission Valley in either 1821 or 1822, according to Roy Grimes's *300 Years in Victoria County*. She settled down in present-day Victoria County and began ranching.

"She was born Marquerite Theresa Robertson in New Orleans in 1789, of an English father and a French mother, and she died in Victoria on Oct. 21, 1878, and is buried in Evergreen Cemetery," Wolff wrote in a 1985 *Victoria Advocate* column.

Wolff goes on to explain, however, that a fifth-generation descendant of Wright "has determined without a doubt that this pioneer woman then known as Marquerite Trudeau didn't arrive in Texas until 1825 and on the Guadalupe by the end of 1826."

It is generally accepted, though, as Blanche de Leon pointed out, that Wright was here before Martin de Leon. "There is no question that when Don Martin de Leon arrived with his first colonists in 1824 she was already here," Grimes noted.

De Leon accepted her as a colonist, just as he accepted John Linn and others already in the vicinity, granting Wright a "league of land under Mexican law, 4,428 acres, and the additional labor, 177 acres."

She was not a handsome woman, Wolff explained. "[She] was a rather rough looking woman," he wrote. "She did have a hard life."

She was widowed twice before coming to Victoria and then married De Leon colonist John David Wright of Tennessee. Apparently, life with John David Wright was difficult and often painful for her. She alleged in divorce proceedings that he killed her son, Peter Hayes, and "[contended] she had been abused, threatened and otherwise maltreated by her husband," Grimes noted.

John David Wright also claimed her headright without her knowledge, effectively stealing her land out from under her. She learned of it in 1836, the same year she became the "Little Mother of Texas."

After the Palm Sunday 1836 massacre of Colonel James Walker Fannin and his troops, several escaped Texian soldiers were successfully hidden by Margaret Wright.

She said her husband was nowhere to be found during this period, from 1835 to 1842. This includes the time—1836—when King said she hid the soldiers in her skirt to keep them from General Urrea's Mexican forces.

Despite being a hero of the Texas Revolution and at one time owning and operating a large ranching enterprise in Mission Valley, Wright died in destitution.

A September 14, 1876 article in the *Victoria Advocate*, then edited by Edward Linn, pleaded her cause:

> *We are informed that Mrs. Margaret Wright, an old and respected citizen of this city, is now suffering for the want of proper care at home in the middle part of town. Mrs. Wright is connected with the early history of our town, coming here among the first American settlers, some 50 years ago. She is now old and feeble, and her condition excites the pity of all. We suggest that the town authorities pay some attention to this matter and give her aid required by this helpless person.*

To imagine this pioneer woman, alone on the frontier, caring for five children by herself while starting a ranch, as "helpless" is a sad outcome. She outlived at least two of her seven children. She had two with John David Wright, in addition to the five she already had.

The Victoria committee for the Texas Sesquicentennial (1986) selected Wright as a pioneer to be honored, Wolff wrote in 1984, making special note of the name bestowed upon her by Houston.

The History and Heritage of Victoria County by the Victoria County Genealogical Society, a multivolume text on hand at the Victoria Regional History Center, noted that the Heller family later acquired much of Wright's ranching lands. Raymond Wesley Heller, born in 1926, told chroniclers "his parents bought a 316-acre farm from the Woffords and Mary Willis Jackson, and [we moved] on the Lower Mission Valley Road. The property was part of several thousand acres that Margaret Wright ran cattle on and is recognized as the first ranch in Texas."

JOHN JOSEPH "JUAN" LINN

Like the hometown he adopted, John Joseph Linn, one of Victoria's original colonists, was an ever-evolving figure—father of fourteen children, Victoria's first mayor and a merchant, politician, soldier and historian. He was also as complicated as the times he inhabited. He was an immigrant, at first unlawfully in Texas. He was an intense patriot, loyal to the De Leon colony and to Texas, but not to every government the two resided under. He was a freedom fighter, and he held people in bondage.

Most of all, found in the pages of his own reminiscences, is a man who loved Victoria, Texas and the De Leon family, speaking admirably of Silvestre, one of Empresario Don Martin de Leon's sons. The foremost scholar on the De Leon family, Carolina Castillo Crimm, said Linn helped Doña Patricia de Leon flee Texas when the remnants of the founding family were exiled for several years.

He was lovingly called "Juan" by the Mexican colonists in Victoria.

On the corner of Bridge and Juan Linn Streets, next to the Victoria Police Department, sits a historic marker honoring the beloved Victoria colonial. The marker is across the street from Linn's homesite. He died there in 1885.

Linn was born on June 19, 1798, in County Antrim, Ireland, according to the *Handbook of Victoria County*, on hand at the Victoria Regional History Center. His father, John Linn, a college professor, had to flee Ireland after participating in the Irish rebellion of 1798. He was branded a traitor by the British but escaped to New York.

John Joseph Linn was apprenticed at the age of sixteen to a merchant and later "established his own merchant business in New Orleans in 1822 and became interested in Texas during business trips to Mexico," Craig H. Roell wrote in the *Handbook* article. Linn had his sights set on the De Leon colony. Martin de Leon "needed additional colonists," Crimm wrote in *De Leon: A Tejano Family History*.

"Among the later arrivals were the Carbajal family and the four Benavides brothers," Crimm noted. "De Leon also found sixteen Anglo-American families who had already moved into the area illegally, including John Linn, John D. Wright, and Joseph Ware." De Leon accepted these men, Crimm wrote, making the Victoria colony remarkably inclusive.

One Mexican official who visited the colony in 1828 "indicated that there were individuals in the Victoria colony from Canada, the United States, Ireland, France and Germany. Unlike Austin's settlements on the Colorado, Martin de Leon's colony was, by necessity, multicultural from its inception," Crimm wrote. The Mexican authorities did not all "approve of the varied ethnic flavor of the Victoria colony," Crimm noted.

Linn was one of those varied flavors, but at heart he was, above all else, a Texian. He appreciated the beauty of his adopted homeland. "In travelling from Corpus Christi to Victoria I was delighted with the appearance of the country," Linn wrote in his *Reminiscences of Fifty Years in Texas*. "It was

John Joseph "Juan" Linn's gravesite at Evergreen Cemetery.

in the last days of April, and the landscape was rendered charming by the profusion of many-colored wildflowers that greeted the eyes on all sides."

Linn received land grants in both the De Leon and Power settlements, according to Roell, but kept his residence and business in Victoria. "I purchased a lot fronting the public square in Victoria and caused the framework of a house to be erected, of cypress timber, of which a quantity was then to be had in the bottom south of town," Linn wrote. "This house was completed in 1831, and I have continued to reside in it up to the present date [1883]."

Once Texas declared its intention to seek independence from Mexico, Linn was all in. "Linn was intensely loyal to Texas and the De Leon colony and was among the first to oppose [Mexican president and commander] Antonio Lopez de Santa Anna," Roell noted.

Linn wrote that after Santa Anna's capture by Sam Houston, Linn himself spoke with the Mexican president in captivity.

Linn was elected the first mayor of Victoria on April 16, 1839. He served in the Second and Third Congresses of the Republic of Texas.

"By 1850, at age 52, Linn had $20,000 in property, and the 1860 census listed him as owning seven slaves," Roell wrote.

Linn's son, John Jr., fought for the Confederacy and died at Brownsville, Roell wrote.

In 1883, Linn published his memoir, *Reminiscences of Fifty Years in Texas*. The Texas State Historical Association suggests that Linn's dear friend and admirer Victor Rose ghostwrote the book but noted the story is authentically Linn's.

Of note in the book is a delightful description of Victoria's first jail:

> *In the year 1843 or 1844 it was concluded that Victoria had attained to that degree of enlightenment that demanded a jail in which evil-doers could be confined. It was constructed of hewn logs, about a foot square, and pinned together by wooden pins. Between the door and one corner a log four and a half feet long was fastened to the jamb of the door by an iron spike. The building was soon occupied by two evil-doers, who readily observed that the wooden pins constituted the key of the position.*

Those first two convicts escaped, Linn noted.

Linn lived through the greatest changes in Victoria, as did Wright, from its birth as a Mexican colony to its time as a city in the Republic of Texas, to annexation by the United States, then secession to a Confederate state and back to an American state again and for all time since.

Found in the rich story of Wright's and Linn's lives is the story of Victoria.

Chapter 3

A TRIP TO MEXICO CITY WITH A DE LEON DESCENDANT

As the bicentennial year dawned and Victoria prepared to celebrate our shared Hispanic heritage, I was invited on a trip to Mexico City with three De Leon descendants, a leading De Leon scholar and a host of other historians. What I learned shed light on the reason for the shortage of knowledge, outside of Victoria, of our founding family's immense contribution to the story of Texas.

And, after all, many of the De Leon forebears certainly began their American journey in what is now the megalopolis of Mexico City.

A DECEMBER MEETING

Back in December 2023, as we closed in on the bicentennial year, I met Blanche de Leon at the Victoria Public Library, where she was processing an applicant to the Daughters of the Republic of Texas.

She said she had an old history book that belonged to her family, if I would like to look at it. Of course, I did. The book was incredibly old, falling apart at the binding, but the pages inside were still legible; however, the cover and title page were worn, and I could not make out the name of the book. Once I started reading the pages, I quickly realized, to my delight, that she had an old edition of Victor Marion Rose's *Some Historical Facts in Regard to the Settlement of Victoria, Texas: Its Progress and Present Status*, published in 1883, nearly sixty years after Victoria was founded. A copy of the book was placed in a time capsule and put in the cornerstone of the Victoria County Courthouse, completed about ten years after its publication.

I gingerly turned the pages of the old book with a rubber-tipped pointer, wondering how many other people, important to our history, had perused this very book. Certainly, several descendants of our founders had read this copy.

After I looked through the book, Blanche and I visited for a few minutes. She mentioned that she would be going to Mexico City in late January/early February 2024 on a tour with Ana Carolina Castillo Crimm and that I should come along. Crimm authored *De Leon: A Tejano Family History*, and I cite her often in my work. Along with A.B.J. Hammett's *The Empresario Don Martin de Leon*, Crimm's work provides the most complete history of Victoria's founding family.

I politely declined the invitation, deeply disappointed and thinking at the moment that I could not afford such a venture.

Crimm owns Historic Tours of Texas, based in Huntsville. Some of the company's tours dip deep down into Mexico, which makes sense when you consider that Texas's and Mexico's histories are intertwined.

The tour Blanche invited me to attend was in honor of a little-known hero of the American Revolution, a Spaniard named Bernardo de Galvez. Galvez fought the British along the southern coast during our Revolution and was governor of the Spanish province of Louisiana and later a popular viceroy in Mexico, among his many other accolades. He captured British forts in Louisiana and Florida, helping defeat English forces.

The mention of Galvez piqued my interest. After all, this is the man for whom Galveston is named. Why, I wondered, had I never learned about him? Certainly, I had learned about the French general Marquis de Lafayette.

I have studied history for nearly forty years, voraciously reading every book I could. I spent eight years in college as an undergraduate and graduate student. All of this, and I had never heard of Galvez's contributions to our independence up to that point, much as I had never heard of Martin de Leon before coming to Victoria eight years ago. Here was another neglected chapter of our common story. Another important figure fills a background of shadows.

For example, in the case of Martin de Leon, he was one of only two successful empresarios in Texas's history. His misfortune, in this instant, was that the other was Stephen F. Austin, the Father of Texas. So, to Austin, De Leon would take a backseat—a place in Austin's long shadow, so to speak.

The De Leon family, a Mexican family of Spanish descent, not only founded Victoria, but they were also instrumental in Texas's bid for independence, smuggling weapons, supplying horses and cattle and even fighting alongside Juan Seguín and other heroes of the revolution.

As the historian Thomas Chavez of New Mexico, author of eleven history books, explained to me, there exists a deeply rooted bias against the "Catholic Spanish," and so against Mexico, pervasive in our story. This plays out in the fact that the De Leon family was exiled following the revolution, cruelly evicted from the town they founded based on nothing more than their country of origin, even though they were thorough-going Texans. The De Leon family even had the first cattle brand in Texas. You do not get much more Texan than that.

Well, I know what happened to the De Leon family, and I have written plenty about it. Now, I thought, perhaps I could learn more about why it happened the way it did by getting myself to Mexico City with Blanche and Dr. Crimm and learning about this other mostly overlooked Spaniard who is key to the story of Texas and the United States.

I managed to pull together the funds and set off with Blanche and a group of about fifteen other historical adventurers on January 31. Incidentally, at least three of them were descended from De Leons. It seemed to me there could be no better time to embrace our Spanish heritage at its roots.

THE TRAVELERS

The group who gathered in Mexico City was made up of academics, historians all along the spectrum of experience. While Blanche is very humble and does not like to be considered a historian, a historian is exactly what she is: keeper and commentator of her family's story. The group included her cousin Rosemarie de Leon–Garcia. She grew up in Victoria but moved to Albuquerque, New Mexico, years later. She worked as a paralegal interpreter for the courts there until she retired. She said of her De Leon forebears, "They were humble. It was in their nature to be humble and treat others with respect."

Another traveler, Gustavo "Gus" N. Hinojosa, of Dallas, shares an ancestor with Blanche and Rosemarie, making them distant cousins. He is the president of the Mexican American Museum of Texas, a fledgling organization whose purpose is "to provide, permanently and on a visiting basis, a venue for exhibiting or interpreting Mexican American history, culture, and origins, as well as past and present customs." Hinojosa is a well-spoken man with a quick sense of humor and a palpable passion for his heritage. The museum, he said, is a work in progress, having pop-ups around Texas and hoping for a permanent home. His will be the first such museum in a state once exclusively occupied by Mexicans.

If you think about it, even Stephen F. Austin was a Mexican. Indeed, he was at one time a loyal citizen of said country and urged others to practice the fidelity he modeled.

Thomas E. Chavez was also among the group. He earned his doctorate in history from the University of New Mexico. His résumé includes a posting as the executive director of the National Hispanic Culture Center in Albuquerque, New Mexico. "Before that, he was Director of the Palace of Governors in Santa Fe, New Mexico, for twenty-one years," noted a flier for the tour. Chavez was a literal fount of knowledge, speaking with casual ease about complicated subjects in history. His excitement for and interest in the past flowed from him as he spoke. Listening to him, I almost felt he was a witness to history. I immediately felt I could trust his depth of knowledge.

Also in the group was Sandra Arce Lopez, currently of Angleton but originally from the Rio Grande Valley. She is president of the Hispanic Genealogical Society of Houston. She was friendly and easy to talk with, sharing my enthusiasm for the trip.

Others in the group included Richard and Merilee Espinosa, John Espinosa, Scot MacRae, Jill Brooks, Ellen Norton and Andy Savage. Additionally, Blanche de Leon's good friend Norma Rojas, of Goliad, was along for the journey.

And lastly was a pair of dynamic sisters, Mary Anthony Long Startz and Molly Long Fernandez de Mesa. Molly's Spanish husband, Luis Fernandez de Mesa, accompanied her. Luis was a gentleman cut from a chivalric cloth, always debonair and exceedingly polite. Startz lives in Houston, where she "serves as Governor of the Houston chapter of the order of Granaderos y Damas de Galvez, working to promote the history of Spain's role in the American Revolution."

Each of the travelers on this journey, except myself and Rosemarie, was either Granaderos or Damas de Galvez. The sisters Long were easy to talk with and were ever eager to share their knowledge, which they possessed in ready abundance.

Now that I have introduced my touring companions, I would like to pause and discuss the opening of Crimm's book on the De Leon family. She begins the first chapter with a mention of none other than Bernardo de Galvez. She describes a young Martin de Leon, in 1780, "gangly with the new growth of his fourteen years," racing home to beg of his father that he might join De Galvez's military exploits.

"[Martin] assured himself that as a grown man of fourteen, he could certainly join Don Bernardo's military expedition against British West Florida and its capital at Pensacola," Crimm wrote. "Little else was discussed in the plazas and homes of northern New Spain. The courageous commandant [De Galvez] had launched brilliant attacks up the Mississippi and swept the British from their forts at Natchez, Baton Rouge, and Manchac."

Of course, young Martin did not join De Galvez. "Martin's father insisted that he remain at his studies," Crimm noted. He would survive into adulthood to journey north with his family, to the Guadalupe River, as we know.

"The De Leons were always on the move," Blanche said during the trip. "They always moved to unfamiliar places. They moved around Spain, and when that was not enough, they came to New Spain and pushed out into the northern frontier here."

As for De Galvez, he was key to the United States' victory over Great Britain during the Revolution. Thomas Chavez said at one point, he had gone up to Boston to give a lecture about De Galvez's key contributions to U.S. independence.

"Well, these northeasterners didn't want to hear about how a Spaniard helped win the War for Independence," he said. "So, I told them that Washington personally thanked Spain for helping him win the war. I asked them if Washington was wrong. That ended it."

Now, back to Mexico City.

DAY ONE: FEBRUARY 1, 2024

On our first day in Mexico City, we went to Chapultepec Castle. In 1785, Viceroy Bernardo de Galvez commanded the construction of a regal home for himself on Chapultepec Hill. The hill rises above the city, and the castle, finished long after De Galvez died, now houses the Mexican National Museum of History. On a side note, the flag of the New Orleans Greys, captured by Santa Anna at the Alamo, is housed in a glass case in the museum. Chapultepec was also the site of the Battle of Chapultepec, the battle for Mexico City, during the Mexican-American War.

Most students of American history know that the war was won at the decisive Chapultepec battle on September 12–13, 1847, fought by young West Pointers who would later become famous American Civil War generals.

A mural on the ceiling of one entryway to Chapultepec Castle in Mexico City.

Chapultepec was the Mexican military academy at the time, defended by young cadets housed there.

As I walked into the castle, my eyes were drawn to a mural on the ceiling above me. Depicted in bright colors, a young Mexican cadet, draped in a flag, falls from the sky, a look of sad desperation on his face. Surrounding him in outlined relief are scenes of battle—men, artillery wheels, horses and the castle walls swirl above and about the falling boy. The American flag rises above him to one side. An eagle, the Mexican symbol of nationality, flies above him. He represents one of six young cadets who leapt to their deaths as the battle was lost. Rather than see the Mexican flag captured, he grasped it and jumped to his death.

Here I was faced with the other side of the story—the Mexican side, seen in the sorrow of forlorn loss in the face of a young man about to die.

Flag of the New Orleans Greys, taken by Mexican troops at the Alamo on March 6, 1836, on display at the National Museum in Mexico City.

As I walked into the room that housed the flag captured at the Alamo, I was met with the words "Secesion texana (1836)." And, for the first time, I saw from the Mexican perspective that our Texas Revolution was an illegal Texas secession for them. Texas seceded twice, I realized, once from Mexico, successfully, and once from the United States, without the same result. It is all a matter of perspective, and I was in the home of the Mexican story.

In another room in the castle, portraits of all the Spanish viceroys (there were many) hang, including one of Bernardo de Galvez and another of his father. A large, dark equestrian painting of Bernardo graces a strikingly yellow wall at the end of the hall of portraits. It seems he was one of the most famous viceroys. He was certainly the only one who garnered such a large equestrian addition.

After visiting Chapultepec, our group went to the center of Mexico City, to the recently unearthed ruins of the main Aztec pyramid at Tenochtitlan.

A sixteenth-century cathedral rises toward the sky across the way from the remains of the pyramid. Inside the cathedral, ornate paintings and statues of Catholic saints awash in rich colors stand guard, ready to receive contemplations and prayers. In the cathedral's nearly five centuries of existence, I wondered how many millions of prayers were sent heavenward from inside its thick walls.

Outside, Aztec Indians performed traditional cleansings in the plaza, with the burning of sage and the blowing of conches. The Aztecs were there about one hundred years before the Spanish. The Spanish ruled New Spain for about three hundred years after destroying the Aztec empire. Then, the Mexicans, who take their name from the Aztecs, threw off the Spanish and, later, the French.

DAY TWO: FEBRUARY 2

On our second full day in Mexico City, we attended the "Symposium on Spain and the War for American Independence: 'Opening Doors to Revolutionary War Ancestors!'"

The conference was at the Casino Español de Mexico, a castle-like building with marble floors and regal adornments on every wall. The Spanish consulate general in Mexico, Manuel Hernández y Ruigómez, born in 1955, attended, met with and spoke to our group. Other speakers included Crimm, the Long sisters and Chavez. The master of ceremonies was John Espinosa.

"[Galvez] is the leader of the country [New Spain]. He is 39 years old," Crimm said. "He has these new enlightenment ideas. Bernardo de Galvez loved and encouraged the theater. The people saw him in the theater, but he wasn't hanging out at the church. He believed that the theater was a way to educate. He believed in a level of equality. These were scandalous ideas."

Crimm noted that Galvez cared about the people of Mexico, insisting they be fed during a drought and even paying for the burial of a peasant who died on the street. When he died, the people of New Spain deeply mourned the death of this compassionate leader, Crimm said.

Before he was viceroy, he was a military commander. Chavez explained how De Galvez, with the backing and planning of his friend Francisco Saavedra, helped the American colonies defeat the British during the

The Spanish consulate general in Mexico, Manuel Hernández y Ruigómez, with Blanche de Leon in Mexico City, February 2, 2024.

American Revolution, winning fights against the British on our southern shores. Saavedra, Chavez said, even obtained funding for the French naval support at the Battle of Yorktown, ultimately securing American independence.

In speaking of Spain's contributions to the American Revolution, the Long sisters mentioned that the king of Spain, Carlos III, "issued a royal decree in 1780 that every Spanish citizen was requested to donate two pesos and every Indian and mestizo to donate one peso. They were a voluntary donation toward the war effort," called a *donativo*. In this way, Mexico (New Spain) contributed to American victory in the American Revolution, just as they also contributed to the Northern victory during the American Civil War.

At the same time as the American Civil War (1861–65), Mexican troops defeated French forces at the May 5, 1862 Battle of Puebla, thus maintaining their independence and thwarting French plans to aid Confederate forces from Mexico. For this, they received the written gratitude of President Abraham Lincoln, just as the Spaniards in Mexico had received General George Washington's expressed gratitude. Twice, Mexico helped the United States win wars—one for independence and one for "a new birth of freedom."

And yet, as Chavez pointed out, we are less likely to hear of these contributions because of an Anglo bias in the relaying of American history. This is the same bias that gives precedence to Austin over De Leon, the same bias that saw the expulsion of the De Leon family after Texas secured its independence from Mexico.

After the symposium, about half the attendees went to the Basilica of Our Lady of Guadalupe. Here, we saw the *tilma*, Juan Diego's rough cloak bearing an image of Mary, who is said to have appeared miraculously on a hill just above the cathedral.

Recall now that Martin de Leon named Victoria "La Nuestra Señora de Guadalupe de Jesus" in honor of Our Lady of Guadalupe. The name was only later changed to Guadalupe Victoria and then simply Victoria. Our Lady of Guadalupe is the patroness of the Americas and is also where our river gets its name.

DAY THREE: FEBRUARY 3

On Saturday, our third full day in Mexico City, we traveled to the Coyoacán area of the city. This is where Frida Kahlo's famous blue house is located. Here, we saw the exterior of her studio, connected by a bridge to Diego Rivera's studio. Rivera was a famous muralist and twice Kahlo's husband.

Certainly, I thought, these are the two famous ladies of Mexico, Frida and Our Lady of Guadalupe. It is their images I found everywhere in the city, decorating everything from walls to handbags and keychains.

We strolled around an artists' market in Coyoacán. Kahlo's image was everywhere, in bright colors on canvas, handbags and jewelry, as was Our Lady of Guadalupe; as she appeared on the tilma, she now appeared on every sort of material, thousands of times over. It is no wonder her revered name was carried to Victoria.

Blanche de Leon
in Mexico City,
February 1, 2024.

DAY FOUR: FEBRUARY 4

This would be my final day in Mexico City.

Bernardo de Galvez died a rather young man, in 1786, after serving about one year as viceroy. He is buried in Mexico City in the San Fernando Cathedral. Here, the group of Granaderos y Damas laid a wreath in honor of this little-known Revolutionary War Patriot—deep in the heart of Mexico.

GETTING THE STORY OF VICTORIA'S FOUNDING OUT THERE

This is where Blanche comes in. She has worked tirelessly to see her family restored to its place in history. Throughout the trip, she engaged people with the story of Victoria's founding and information about the upcoming bicentennial celebrations.

She brought along buttons and stickers bearing the De Leon cattle brand with the words "First Cattle Brand in Texas—Martin de Leon—Victoria,

TX—Espiritu De Jesus—1807" surrounding the symbol, as well as colorful metal pins celebrating two hundred years of Victoria history with the city's bicentennial logo. She handed these out to all the members of our party.

So, here we were, Blanche and I, nearly 1,300 miles from Victoria, deep in the country of Victoria's De Leon origin, sharing the De Leon story with other historians engaged in embracing Mexican heritage in Texas and the United States.

Yes, Austin is important to the story of Texas, but so is Martin de Leon. And certainly he is of premier importance to the story of Victoria.

Chapter 4

THE CHAPEL AND OTHER TEJANO TRADITIONS

At the February 2024 lecture she gave at the Victoria Public Library, Blanche de Leon shared what she called a "bit of juicy information" with the audience: she revealed to the audience what the bicentennial statue of founder Martin de Leon is pointing at.

The statues, which were cast in bronze at a foundry north of San Antonio, are of Martin and Patricia de Leon, Victoria's founders. They were revealed amidst much fanfare on April 13, 2024, in De Leon Plaza, on the 200th anniversary of the city's founding.

She explained to the audience at the lecture that Martin is pointing toward the site of the "grand cathedral" he will build for Patricia in the new colony.

"Of all the community-oriented buildings on the Tejano ranch, the chapel had the loftiest appeal to Tejano ideals on the frontera," Andrés Tijerina wrote in *Tejano Empire: Life on the South Texas Ranchos*.

Having had two ranches, likely with small ranch or home chapels, in South Texas before his empresarial grant was approved, it was Martin's "dream," Blanche said, to build a proper chapel for Patricia and his colony. The dream has been incorporated into the commemorative statues.

Tijerina's book gives the reader a glimpse into the lives of Tejanos like the De Leon family. "The chapel, *la capilla*," he wrote, "was an integral element of the early Tejano ranch long before missionaries arrived."

Many of these South Texas ranchos were built by Tejano families on land granted to them by Spain, and later Mexico, just as Martin de Leon received land after his service in the military. For many ranchos, the land they worked had been in their family for decades. "Thus, when Tejanos worshipped, they prayed to their own patron saints, on land their fathers gave them, and on an altar they built with their own hands," Tijerina wrote.

Patricia de Leon brought a golden monstrance with her to Victoria, Blanche said, and it can be viewed at St. Mary's Catholic Church, the descendant and fulfillment of Martin's dream. Patricia and her daughters also "embroidered beautiful linens for the altar," Blanche added.

"Religion was a major part of Tejano ethnicity—a way of demonstrating a distinct difference from the ever-growing number of Anglo Americans moving into South Texas," Tijerina wrote.

Patricia de Leon's life was likely steeped in prayer, as many Tejano families like hers observed vespers, or nightly prayers, prescribed by the Catholic Church. "Vespers was a tradition on many ranches. Each evening, led by the patriarch and matriarch, the entire family knelt and prayed: 'Ave Maria, madre de Dios, Llena eres de gracia, Ruega por nosotros…'" Tijerina wrote.

Tejanos were demonstrative in their religious practices, often having elaborate processions with gun salutes honoring saints or Our Lady of Guadalupe. Their altars were of particular pride for the Tejanas, who decorated them with strips of fabric, flowers and candles, Tijerina noted.

"Tejanos prayed aloud, chanting in unison, and often staged formal processions through the courtyard as they chanted," he wrote.

The conservative Catholic Church grew uncomfortable with these pageantries in later years and appointed French priests to the area to bring about a more formal structure. In 1847, two or three years before Patricia de Leon died, "Jean Marie Odin, of Lyons, France, [who] was appointed bishop of the Texas diocese of Galveston…assigned the Rev. James Giraudon to Victoria," Tijerina wrote.

CROSSES ON THE SIDE OF THE ROAD

One can hardly drive down a Texas highway these days without noticing sentinel reminders of loss—crosses posted in the grass, marking the site of a death. This tradition also has its roots in Tejano religious practices, according to Tijerina.

"For most Tejanos, death came on the ranch or while they were working or traveling in the chaparral," he wrote. "Tejanos had a tradition of marking a place of death with a cross along the roadside, and travelers through Texas reported roadside crosses as early as 1829, when an official crossed from Mexico City into Texas at Mier on the Rio Grande."

Anglo travelers, once welcomed on South Texas ranchos, also experienced delicious bits of Tejano culture for the first time.

THE TORTILLA: THE STUFF OF LIFE

When Frederick Law Olmsted, a journalist and landscape artist, traveled through Texas during the mid-nineteenth century, he first encountered tacos while dining with a Tejano ranch family in South Texas, Tijerina noted.

Olmsted wrote, "Our first difficulty was the absence of fork or spoon, but we soon learned the secret of twisting a tortilla into a substitute, and disposed of a hearty meal." Olmsted went on to write that the tortilla was "decidedly superior to the southern corn 'pone,'" Tijerina wrote. Tejanas, like Patricia de Leon and her daughters, prepared tortillas each day.

"Historical accounts indicate that Tejanas kept tortillas, a pot of frijoles, and a pot of coffee on the fire most of the day," Tijerina wrote. "The tortilla was simple, but it represented much more than just food. It was the stuff of Tejano life."

ORIGIN OF THE TEN-GALLON HAT

Vaqueros, the original cowboys, worked cattle and mustangs on South Texas ranchos. Martin de Leon produced marketable horses from 128 mustangs he purchased at La Bahia in 1807, during his earlier ranching venture, Ana Carolina Castillo Crimm wrote in *De Leon: A Tejano Family History*.

"With good brood mares and the donkeys his wife had received as her dowry, combined with his experience as a muleteer, he could also breed mules for the many mule trains coming and going in Texas," Crimm wrote.

Martin de Leon would have employed vaqueros to work his livestock. The Tejano gentleman, like De Leon, wore a broad-brimmed hat while overseeing his herds, predecessor of the cowboy hat so famous now in Texas.

"The patriarch wore a Tejano hat, which today is called simply a 'cowboy hat,'" Tijerina wrote. "The crown was decorated with a gold chain or with several silver coins or decorative disks called galones. The hat accommodated about ten disks around the brim, leading to the English term 'ten gallon hat.'"

WHERE DID ALL THE RANCHOS GO?

Richard King and Mifflin Kenedy, two wealthy Anglo ranchers, sent out groups of irregular Texas Rangers to terrorize South Texas rancheros and their families, causing many to flee to the safety of towns south of the Rio Grande, Tijerina wrote. Once the families were gone, Anglo ranchers would consume their lands.

Fernando de Leon, Martin's oldest son, "lost 50,000 acres to sheriffs' auctions after he was driven out of Victoria after the Texas Revolution," Tijerina wrote, citing Crimm. When he returned to Victoria in 1846, he successfully defended another 50,000 acres through litigation, Tijerina wrote. Fernando was fortunate.

"The Anglo capitalist ranchers used their lawyers to perfect the land titles and preclude future lawsuits that might question their acquisition of these lands," Tijerina wrote. "They then justified the acquisition of Tejano lands because, notwithstanding the violence and sheriff's auctions, it was 'legal.'"

One collection of Tejano land titles was even lost in a shipwreck off the coast of Texas. Those Tejano rancheros then had to prove the legitimacy of their land claims, Tijerina wrote.

Historian David Montejano described the position of the Tejano eloquently in a lecture he gave during a 1991 Texas State Historical Association conference in San Antonio. The lecture is published in the book *Mexican Americans in Texas History*.

Montejano compares the plight of the Tejano people to that of the Palestinian people. Once Anglo Americans wrested Texas from Mexico, South Texas rancheros were in a kind of limbo, like the Palestinian Israelis. Slowly, the Tejanos were dispossessed of their ancestral homes and displaced by a "chosen people." In the case of South Texas, the Anglo Americans were the chosen ones. After all, the Alamo is called the "shrine of Texas liberty." A shrine is a holy place associated with a sacred person. The Alamo had a trinity.

It became "a powerful story line for Texas historians: the prevailing image, according to a recent review of the literature, became one of 'sure shooting, morally upright frontiersmen' against 'blood thirsty and tyrannical Mexicans,'" Montejano said.

Tejanos were made foreigners and enemies on lands their families had possessed for decades before Anglos settled in Texas, just as the De Leon family was forced out of the town they founded and had to flee the fledgling Republic of Texas, in fear of their lives.

In this borderland the Tejanos occupied—south of the Nueces River and north of the Rio Grande—so precarious was their situation that they even considered trying to break off and start a country of their own, Tijerina wrote.

"During the years of the Texas Republic, the Mexicans north of the Rio Grande were attacked by Anglos as well as by Mexican armies," Tijerina wrote.

Federalist leaders in the area, including none other than Jose Maria Jesus Carbajal, a De Leon son-in-law and the surveyor of Victoria, frustrated by it all, plotted "to organize an armed insurrection and declare an Independent Republic of the Rio Grande."

So caught in the middle, quite literally, were they, between the country of their origin and the new state. And yet, it was they who had changed the wild frontera of South Texas into a ranching kingdom.

"Tejanos founded the ranching frontier on their land grants, and thus were not only leaders of their South Texas communities but also founders of the state of Texas," Tijerina wrote.

Martin de Leon and his family are such founders.

Chapter 5

VICTORIA IN EARLY WARTIME

ONE DE LEON GRANDCHILD
UNFAIRLY MALIGNED

Martin and Patricia de Leon's children would bear them about twenty-two grandchildren, many of whom lived in the Victoria area. Most were landowners, recouping family land after the Texas Revolution–era exile. Some earned reputations as rowdies. Almost all endured "racist sneers," Crimm wrote.

One grandson, Silvestre, fought for the Confederacy during the American Civil War and was taken prisoner. He suffered terribly in a Northern prisoner-of-war camp and returned to Victoria a broken man. He died within four years of his release. In an era when post traumatic stress disorder went unrecognized, he was unfairly branded a drunk and no-account. Incredibly, in October 2023, during the Annual Cemetery Tour at Evergreen Cemetery, empty bottles of liquor were strewn about his grave in the Catholic cemetery.

Silvestre de Leon was born to Felix de Leon and Salome Leal. He was one of seven children in the family. His older brother Patricio de Leon married his cousin Librada de Leon Benavides in 1858. This is the line from which Blanche de Leon is descended. Blanche worked closely with the City of Victoria in planning the bicentennial celebrations. Silvestre is a great-great-uncle to Blanche.

"Of all the brothers, only Silvestre De Leon chose combat outside Texas [during the American Civil War]," Crimm wrote. "Silvestre, now twenty-six, joined Company A of Waller's 13th Cavalry Battalion. Led by Captain James P.B. January, a veteran of the Texas Revolution and Mexican war."

The unit formed at Garcitas Creek, Crimm noted. From there, they marched to Louisiana in the summer of 1862.

"Silvestre and his unit soon had all the glory they cared for," Crimm wrote. "They fought Union forces throughout Louisiana in a series of short, bitter, bloody battles."

New Orleans was captured by Union troops on April 24, 1862, and Waller's men harassed Northern troops and schooners nearby, Donald S. Frazier wrote in *Fire in the Cane Field: The Federal Invasion of Louisiana and Texas, January 1861–January 1863*.

"Late [on the afternoon of September 7, 1862], thirty of Waller's bolder men decided to ride down the levee toward New Orleans and attack a large ship rumored to be aground near Algiers," Frazier wrote. A game of cat-and-mouse ensued in which Waller's troops soon became the mouse, hiding from Union troops in tall sugarcane, hoping for an opportunity to attack.

"Unable to bear the suspense, one man succumbed to buck fever. The tenderfoot discharged his weapon, blowing the Texas ambush," Frazier wrote. Now, the Union troops had the advantage and "thrashed" Waller's men.

"Outnumbered and with their cover blown, Waller's men would have to try to outrun the Federals," Frazier noted. The thirty troopers ran back toward their compatriots, including Silvestre and the bulk of the unit. Captain January refused to skedaddle, and with fifty of his men, he turned to face the pursuing Union troops. Silvestre de Leon stood his ground among these fifty. After "putting on a brave show," they surrendered, Frazier continued. The place of their surrender was called Bonnet Carre. And here, Silvestre's time as a soldier ended and his time as a prisoner began.

"While the rest of his unit gained laurels by defeating Union General Nathanial Banks at Mansfield and at Pleasant Hill, Silvestre suffered through the remainder of the war in a Union prisoner of war camp without sufficient food, clothing, or shelter," Crimm wrote, "conditions common to all the Civil War prisons." De Leon returned to Victoria after the war, in 1865, "bitter and demoralized."

"Sil began to drink heavily. He ran up large bills for half-gallon jugs of bourbon with William G. Neely and Company," Crimm wrote. "He sold his land, and the money vanished as he gambled and drank his way through town."

Crimm wrote that Silvestre socialized with "the worst of Victoria's young rowdies," including C.L. Thurmond and C.O. Weller, who owned the gaming table Silvestre frequented. Unfortunately for Silvestre de Leon, PTSD would not be recognized as a disorder, or treated, until more than one hundred years later. Christopher Bergland wrote in a 2024 medical journal article that PTSD sufferers often present "behavioral changes such as engaging in reckless activities." In June 1869, four years after his imprisonment ended, De Leon's body was discovered in the Guadalupe River.

"Some suggested it had been a suicide," Crimm concluded.

VICTORIA IN THE AMERICAN CIVIL WAR

Past the Victoria Mall, out on US 77 North, a smaller than normal historic marker sits lonely next to some power line poles at the edge of an empty lot. The marker is entitled "Victoria" and sums up the town's two-hundred-year history in three sentences.

"Founded in 1824 by Martin de Leon as center of his colony, Mexico's buffer against Comanches. Active in 1836 in support of the Texas War for Independence, and in the Confederate cause during Civil War. Historic trade, cattle, oil and industrial center." It is a squat little marker, dedicated in 1964.

Historian Annette Gordon-Reed recently wrote of Texas, "As for the people, the Cowboy, the Rancher, the Oilman—all wearing either ten-gallon hats or Stetsons—dominate as the embodiments of Texas."

The last sentence of the marker seems to bear out Reed's assessment. And yet, there in the first sentence is the Spanish Founding Father of Victoria—a proud Hispanic heritage here thrives.

In the second sentence sits another embodiment of Texas sentiment who would dominate Texas thought for many decades: the Confederate soldier. As Roy Grimes wrote in his book *300 Years in Victoria County*, "Southern sentiment was still quite tender in Victoria in 1885," two decades after the end of the Civil War. It would remain so for many more years.

When secession was declared in Texas, Victoria followed suit. As Grimes wrote, Victoria had "a large, vested interest in that classification of property": slavery. For example, John Linn, one of the original founders, owned several slaves, according to documents at the Victoria Regional History Center. His sons fought for the Confederacy, one dying during the war.

At the outbreak of the Civil War, three or four miles outside Victoria, newly minted Confederate soldiers from Victoria and the surrounding counties trained at Camp Henry E. McCulloch, named for a Texas Revolution hero. Victoria sent three companies off to fight: Company B, Sixth Texas Infantry;

Company A, Thirteenth Texas Cavalry Battalion; and Company C, Fourth Regiment Texas Mounted Volunteers. John Linn's son Charles Carroll Linn served as a first lieutenant in the latter company and survived the war.

Two Confederate soldiers from Victoria—R.R. Gilbert and Charles Leuschner—wrote of their experiences as part of Company B, Sixth Texas Infantry. Gilbert's writings, as "High Private," appeared in the *Victoria Advocate* and the *Houston Telegraph* and were composed at the start of the war. Gilbert, wrote Grimes, "apparently was a newspaperman who served only a comparatively short" enlistment, poking fun in his reports at army life.

As Grimes wrote, "Gilbert quoted the oath for service in the Confederate army as follows: 'Do you solemnly swear that you will stay in the army as long as the war lasts, and fight to the best of your ability; that you will not growl at your rations, and be content with eleven dollars a month, whether you get them or not, so help you God.'"

Belva Zirjacks, one-time president of the Victoria chapter of the United Daughters of the Confederacy, discovered Charles Leuschner's Civil War diary quite by accident while cleaning out a dusty closet at a historic home. It was subsequently published with accompanying text written by Charles D. Spurlin.

Leuschner served in the Confederate army from beginning to end, captured at the November 30, 1864 Battle of Franklin in Tennessee. That battle was a final effort by General John B. Hood's army to snatch victory from the jaws of defeat. So fierce was the fight that men appeared standing in death—propped up by the bodies surrounding them.

Leuschner wrote that the fight was a back-and-forth chaos. At one point, he captured several "yankey" prisoners but then found himself isolated facing a line of enemy soldiers and had to quit his vocation, throw down his rifle and surrender. He was sent off to a prisoner-of-war camp and on December 21, 1864, wrote, "I got sick with feber." Then, on January 2, 1865, he noted, "I got well."

The final paragraph of Leuschner's diary, written on June 15, 1865, after surrender, is a poignant testament to what he suffered during the war and upon surrendering. It is worth reading in its entirety:

I expectant to be happy, and I was for a little while; but it is not so now, my heart has a whegd thrown upon it which cannot be easily taken off. It pains me. I may forget it for a minute or two, but it will come in my mind again. I try all in the world to be happy and other's that see me think so, but there is something that works in me which I dare not explain. Had we gained our independence, I would have bin happy. My heart would have leaped for joy, but now it is not so. When I am in the presence of Ladie's, I forget for a little while; but while I am speaking my troubles come into my mind, where at other times I would have Killed myself a laughing. I could not now make a laughing if I was to try my hardest.

One final note: "Victorians were present at Glorieta, Chickamauga, Atlanta, Chattanooga, Mansfield, and Palmetto Ranch; places that millions of people would read about," Grimes wrote over one hundred years after the Civil War ended.

CAMP HENRY E. McCULLOCH

Confederate volunteers from Victoria and several surrounding counties trained at Camp Henry E. McCulloch, about three miles outside town. The low-hanging branches of nearby trees obscure the historic marker dedicated to the camp on US 87 just three-tenths of a mile shy of Zac Lentz Parkway. All that is clearly visible is the pole the marker is affixed to. It stands next to an empty field—a field that is likely a part of an area where hundreds of troops trained early in 1861 to go to war against the Northern states.

Regardless of what motivated these individual men to enlist, they became part of an army raised to defend slavery, according to several historic sources, many available at the Victoria Regional History Center.

"The great majority of immigrants to antebellum Texas came from older southern states (77 percent of household heads in Texas in 1860 were southern born), and many brought their slaves and all aspects of slavery as it had matured in their native states," Randolph B. Campbell wrote in *An Empire for Slavery: The Peculiar Institution in Texas, 1821–1865*. The book was published in 1989 by the Louisiana State University Press and is available at the regional history center.

During the 1850s, slaves accounted for 30 percent of Texas's population, Campbell noted.

"Texas must be a slave country," Stephen F. Austin wrote in the early years of the Republic of Texas. "Circumstances and unavoidable necessity compels it. It is the wish of the people there, and it is my duty to do all I can, prudently, in favor of it. I will do so."

Without slavery, Austin wrote, Texas could not attract the people to make it a land of sugar and cotton plantations and would instead be populated by shepherds and the poor, Campbell noted in his study.

Camp Henry E. McCulloch historic marker on US Highway 87 near Zac Lentz Parkway in Victoria.

Frederick Law Olmsted, the landscape architect who helped design New York's Central Park, and a sometime journalist, was sent by the *New York Times* in the 1850s to travel through Texas and report on his experience. His travel journal, *A Journey through Texas*, is on hand at the history center and offers some insight into Victoria at the time of his journey. Olmsted wrote about several nearby sugar plantations, stretching from Victoria to Seguin, that produced cane of "unusual size, and perfectly developed." He wrote about a particular master who had to berate his slaves to get any work out of them, noting this was in stark contrast to the thrift of German workers recently settled in the Victoria area.

"This is our first reintroduction to negro servants after our German experiences, and the contrast is most striking and disagreeable," Olmsted wrote. "Here were thirty or forty slaves, but not an order could be executed without more reiteration, and threats and oaths." Of course, the German workers were paid for their labors, whereas the "negro servants" were enslaved and uncompensated.

Of the white people inhabiting Victoria, Olmsted noted a blatant prejudice aimed mostly at Mexican townspeople. White Victorians, he said, spoke of the Mexicans as "vermin, to be exterminated." He mentioned a lady of Victoria who told him "Mexicans had no business" being in Victoria—a colony founded by a Spanish Mexican family.

Olmsted, though he shared some of the prejudicial feelings of his time, noted that slavery was the saddest state he ever saw man held to.

When Abraham Lincoln was elected president in 1860, the Southern states seceded one by one. South Carolina left the Union first and sent commissioners to other Southern states to convince them to join the exit. South Carolina congressman John McQueen was sent as a secessionist envoy to Texas.

Historian Edward H. Bonekemper recently wrote of McQueen's address to the Texas secession convention in his book *The Myth of the Lost Cause*. "On February 1, 1861, he told the Texas convention, 'Lincoln was elected by a sectional vote, whose platform…was to be the abolition of slavery upon this continent and the elevation of our own slaves to an equality with ourselves and our children.'"

Bonekemper noted that when Texas seceded the day after McQueen gave his speech to the convention, "McQueen praised their rejection of three distinct enemy classes, Indians, Mexicans, and Abolitionists, and predicted 'that state would never be reunited with non-slaveholding or fanatical people.'"

In addition, Bonekemper wrote, a Louisiana envoy to Texas, George Williamson, explained the two states' position regarding secession. "Louisiana looks to the formation of a Southern confederacy to preserve the blessings of African slavery.…Louisiana and Texas…are both so deeply interested in African slavery that it may be said to be absolutely necessary to their existence."

Campbell wrote of a sort of collective amnesia in Texas about slavery and its importance in the formation of the state. Texas identifies, he wrote, as "essentially western rather than southern. The state thus becomes part of the romantic West, the West of cattle ranches, cowboys, and gunfighters and seemingly less compelling moral issues such as the destruction of the Indians. So long as Texas is not seen as a southern state, its people do not have to face the great moral evil of slavery and the bitter heritage of black-white relations that followed the defeat of the Confederacy in 1865. Texans are thus permitted to escape part of what C. Vann Woodward called the 'burden of Southern History.'"

Nevertheless, Texas, as part of the Confederacy, fought to maintain slavery. Confederate vice president Alexander H. Stevens articulated this fact in his famous Cornerstone Speech, saying the new Southern government rested on the immutability of slavery.

So, those men gathered on the fields south of today's Zac Lentz Parkway more than 160 years ago became part of an army set to defend slavery; however, as philosophers Ryan Holiday and Stephen Hanselman recently wrote, "The Confederate soldiers served 'in simple obedience to duty as they understood it.' Again—they understood wrongly, but it was their genuine understanding, just as Lincoln was genuine when he ended his famous Cooper Union speech by saying, 'Let us, to the end, dare to do our duty as we understand it.'"

VICTORIA IN THE WAR FOR TEXAS INDEPENDENCE

Three groups of Texian soldiers—prisoners of war—marched out of La Presidio la Bahia in Goliad on Palm Sunday 1836. Their Mexican guards were silent, and some of the prisoners noticed the guards carried no provisions, only their weapons. This made the Texians uneasy about their fate.

Perhaps, hoped the prisoners, the guards would march them to the coast to board ships to New Orleans; but one group marched toward Victoria, decidedly not in the direction of the Gulf. That group marched up the road toward Victoria and then was ordered into a field lined by trees and told to kneel. The men reckoned their fate in that moment and heard two separate volleys in the direction of the other groups' marches.

Most of the men refused to kneel and chose to meet their fate standing. In the melee that followed, some escaped and lived to tell others what happened.

In San Jacinto about one month later, as surely every Texan knows, soldiers shouted, "Remember the Alamo! Remember Goliad!" as they handed Mexican general Antonio Lopez de Santa Anna a sound defeat.

The Texian army was only about nine hundred strong at that time, led by Sam Houston.

Victoria was a mostly abandoned town. Most residents fled during the Runaway Scrape—a tide of refugees, fleeing Santa Anna's approaching army. The retreating Mexican army flowed back through the Crossroads, followed, in part, by Thomas Jefferson Rusk's Texian army of about three hundred men. Rusk's army buried the men massacred at Goliad, including their commander, Colonel James W. Fannin.

A bit about Rusk: he became the secretary of war for the newly formed Republic of Texas. He was thirty-four years old in 1836 and a commanding presence by most accounts. "Like many Texas patriots, he was a powerfully

Opposite, top: A reenactor portrays a Texian drummer during the March 23, 2024 reenactment of the Battle of Coleto Creek in Goliad.

Opposite, bottom: Reenactors portray Mexican troops during the reenactment.

Right: Battle of Coleto Creek and Goliad Massacre historic marker at the battleground in Fannin, just north of Goliad.

Below: Fannin Burial Monument Marker in Goliad near Presidio la Bahia.

built man, towering well over six feet tall and well-proportioned: he was every bit as awesome a man as Houston," Bob Boyd wrote in *The Texas Revolution: A Day-by-Day Account*.

Rusk and his army countermarched to Victoria after burying the martyred soldiers at Goliad. Outside town, along the banks of Spring Creek, Rusk's contingent camped and awaited the unfolding of events. He soon received a message from Henry Teal and Henry W. Karnes, both imprisoned at Matamoros. The message was smuggled out in the handle of a whip and warned Rusk the Mexican army was reassembling

Camp Victoria historic marker.

and intended to return to crush what remained of the Texian forces. Rusk sent for help, imploring Texans to stand with his army. He even asked United States forces for assistance.

Soon the camp at Spring Creek—Camp Victoria—swelled to 2,500 Texans, all prepared to fight and secure the San Jacinto victory once and for all. This was the largest gathering of Texans during the revolution. Of course, the Mexican army never returned. But the gathering of soldiers in Victoria impacted the town in positive ways, according to one Welder family ancestor.

"After the disbanding of the Texas army many of the officers remained and sent for their families, giving the town a most charming society. Victoria became a center for amusement and people came from the entire surrounding country for the balls," Mrs. James F. Welder Jr. related in 1936, from stories her mother, an eyewitness to the revolution, told her.

So there, on the corner of Spring Creek Road and Main, now stands a historical marker, designating the place of Camp Victoria. It is a monument to Rusk and the largest Texian assemblage during the Texas Revolution.

One final note: at age fifty-six, Rusk picked up his shotgun, walked out onto the grounds of his farm and shot himself in the head, Boyd wrote.

A TEXAS REVOLUTION HERO'S TROUBLES MIRRORED THOSE OF THE DE LEON FAMILY

Texas was not always so big. As a matter of fact, things in Texas were slight at one point.

When Texas revolted against Mexico in 1835, the state was a remote frontier, bordering what Mexicans then called the United States of the North. Only a handful of towns dotted the state, including Victoria.

The Texian army never reached more than 1,200 volunteers and was usually composed of about half that number. The population of Texas at the time was roughly 35,000 (about half of Victoria's current population), not including Indigenous people.

With such sparse settlement, the De Leon family, the founders of Victoria, loomed large and were among Texas's first families; and yet, in a recent nine-hundred-page publication about Texas history, Martin and Patricia de Leon appear in just three paragraphs, on three separate pages.

Why the scarcity of mention?

One reason can be found in the tragic story of a Tejano hero of the Texas Revolution: Juan Nepomuceno Seguín. Seguín died in Mexico, displaced from his home in San Antonio by fear.

In 1974, his remains returned to Texas and were buried on July 4, 1976, in Seguin, the town named for him, about an hour and a half northwest of Victoria. Seguín's gravesite, at 789 South Saunders Street, lists his many contributions to the Republic of Texas. He fought at the Battle of San Jacinto, served as mayor of San Antonio and was a three-term senator for the Republic of Texas, to name a few. He was one of the first among the famed Texas Rangers.

His father, Erasmo Seguín, and Martin de Leon are mentioned in the same paragraph of that nine-hundred-page history text (*Big Wonderful Thing: A History of Texas* by Stephen Harrington) as early "private rancheros" in the state who employed some of the first Texas cowboys, vaqueros. These Tejano families led the way in Texas history, many embracing later Anglo settlers.

"By the fall of 1834, the most visible Tejano leader was twenty-eight-year-old Juan Seguín, Erasmo's son," historians Bryan Burrough, Chris Tomlinson and Jason Stanford wrote in 2021. "Lean, handsome, and more than a little dashing, Seguín was destined to become the true tragic hero of early Texas."

He married at the age of nineteen to María Gertrudis Flores de Ábrego. The town of Floresville, south of San Antonio, is named for her family. The couple had ten children, the same as Martin and Patricia de Leon.

"Like most of those in the old San Antonio families, Seguín was a liberal federalist who loved Mexico but loathed the authoritarian impulse Santa Anna represented," Burrough, Tomlinson and Stanford added.

As the tide of revolution flowed over the state, Seguín was all-in against Santa Anna and all for Texas. And he was at the Alamo when the show started. Seguín spent most of the thirteen-day siege inside the Alamo but was sent out by Colonel William Barret Travis as a courier, seeking reinforcements, shortly before the place fell to Santa Anna. His story could very well have ended there with Travis, James Bowie and David Crockett, if he had not been sent away. As it was, he was with the Texian army to the end, at San Jacinto on April 21.

Houston did not want Seguín and his mounted troops to fight in the battle, fearing they would be mistaken for Mexican troops and killed by Texian soldiers. Seguín simply had his riders each place a piece of cardboard marked with the words "Recuerden el Alamo!" in their hatbands to distinguish them from Santa Anna's soldados. These "odd bits of cardboard in their hatbands" became "honor badges for their unit," Stephen L. Hardin wrote in *Texian Iliad: A Military History of the Texas Revolution*, on hand at the Victoria Regional History Center.

"Houston avowed that Seguín's 'chivalrous and estimable conduct in the battle won for him my warmest regard and esteem,'" Hardin noted.

Reenactment of the Battle of Coleto Creek at Presidio la Bahia in Goliad, March 23, 2024.

After San Jacinto, Seguín "commanded pursuit of Mexican army remnants," his burial plaque states. He ended up back at the Alamo in 1837, where he honored the fallen. Seguín described the scene in a letter to General Albert Sidney Johnston dated March 13, 1837, as it appears in Timothy M. Matovina's *The Alamo Remembered: Tejano Accounts and Perspectives*:

> *I caused the honors of war to be paid to the remains of the heroes of the Alamo on the 25th of February last. The ashes were found in three heaps. I caused a coffin to be prepared neatly covered with black, the ashes from the two smallest heaps were placed therein and with a view to attach additional solemnity to the occasion were carried to the parish church in Bexar whence it moved with the procession at four o'clock.*

So, how does a Texas hero such as Seguín end up exiled and vilified? Quite frankly, the prejudicial feelings of Anglo Texans after the revolution placed distrust on people of Mexican origin.

"This history would be incomplete, for example, without the troops of Juan Seguín, who played a key role in the rout of Santa Anna at San Jacinto," David Montejano wrote in *Anglos and Mexicans in the Making of Texas, 1836–1986*. "The ambivalence stems rather from the long use of the Alamo as an everyday symbol of the conquest over Mexicans, as a vindication for the repressive treatment of Mexicans."

Or as historians Burrough, Tomlinson and Stanford point out, Tejanos were written out of the story.

Seguín's political rivals trumped up a rabid suspicion that he was loyal to Mexico, and in fear for his life, he left his beloved San Antonio for self-exile in northern Mexico. Mexico, of course, considered him a traitor and offered him two options: prison or military service. He reluctantly took the latter, cementing his supposed betrayal in some Texans' views.

Years later, in 1887, "A representative of the *Laredo Times* called on the venerable Colonel Juan N. Seguín, sole surviving captain of the Texan army participating in the battle of San Jacinto," a *Clarksville Standard* article noted, included in Matovina's study.

Seguín, having been in exile, "inquired of his friends of that period and of their descendants.…As the old veteran inquired of John J. Linn, Edward Linn, John S. Menefee and others, the answer was 'Dead!'" Seguín died three years later, on August 27, 1890, in Nuevo Laredo, Mexico. He was buried there and remained so until 1974, when his remains were returned to Texas.

MEMORIAL SQUARE: A FINAL RESTING PLACE FOR SOLDIERS AND VICTIMS OF DISEASE

Hundreds of bodies are buried beneath a square field on the corner of Commercial and Wheeler Streets, but not one headstone marks a gravesite.

When Victoria was founded, the parcel of land, then at the outside edge of town, was designated a public burial ground. At the time, however, most residents interred their dead in home plots. Still, at least two hundred pioneers and soldiers, many victims of disease and some of execution, are buried beneath Memorial Square.

A historic marker at the site reads, "Once the oldest public burial ground in Victoria. This square was laid out in 1824 when Martin de Leon founded the town then located in the Mexican state of 'Coahuila and Texas.'"

Home burials were deemed a health hazard and outlawed in 1846, and so the cemetery populace grew. It was designated Memorial Square in 1899.

In November 1946, a Victoria County notary public, F.C. Proctor Jr., took a sworn statement from Kate Stoner O'Connor containing a wealth of information about the gravesites. The document is on hand at the history center. O'Connor noted in the statement that she heard her late mother, G.O. Stoner, "tell that many early Victorians were buried in the 'Old Graveyard' now called Memorial Square; and that after this cemetery was closed and Evergreen Cemetery opened, the families could not have their dead re-interred."

She said the reason they could not be moved was because they could not be found for certain. "Headstones or markers of the graves had been knocked down and broken up by the negro soldiers of the United States Army of Occupation who were quartered there in 1865 and 1866," O'Connor stated, "and all traces of the graves were obliterated by these vandals."

A search of documents at the history center, however, gives a fair account of who rests under Memorial Square. First, four of Colonel William Ward's men who were executed by Mexican troops are known to lie beneath the ground in the square. Ward's Georgia Battalion was stationed with Colonel Fannin at Goliad before Fannin's men were massacred by General José Urrea's troops after the Battle of Coleto on March 19 and 20, 1836. The battalion was sent on a raid to Refugio and was later expecting to meet Fannin and his troops in Victoria.

"Ward knew that Fannin had planned to retreat northward to Victoria and sought to rendezvous with him there," Stephen L. Hardin wrote in *Texian Iliad: A Military History of the Texas Revolution*. "By the time they reached the settlement on March 21, however, Urrea already held the town. A number of Ward's men were captured or killed trying to enter town."

Those captured were executed on orders from General Antonio Lopez de Santa Anna. Three of the executed were named by Kate O'Connor in a 1965 letter to Lela Cliburn. Their names were Daniel B. Brooks, Stith Conner and Thomas Quirk. In the same letter, O'Connor wrote that pioneer Peter Underhay Pridham, a veteran of the Battle of San Jacinto, was buried in Memorial Square. Pridham's daughter-in-law was Katie Owens Welder.

She also noted that Confederate soldiers of unknown numbers were laid to rest at Memorial Square.

About fifteen years before the American Civil War, in 1846, Zachary Taylor's American soldiers were en route to Mexico during the Mexican-American War. "They pitched camp at Victoria. While in this vicinity a most terrible epidemic of cholera raged in the ranks of the army," a Daughters of the Republic of Texas document on hand at the history center noted. "Men suffered and died in agony. Their bodies were laid in the consecrated earth of Victoria's old cemetery."

The Daughters of the Republic of Texas, James W. Fannin Chapter, No. 14, dedicated a monument in 1947 on Memorial Square "To the Memory of Texas Soldiers and Victoria Pioneer Families who still lie buried in this sacred soil."

"During the 1846 epidemic people died so fast that coffins could not be constructed fast enough," Gladys Arnold wrote in *The History and Heritage of Victoria County*, "so a mass grave was dug, and bodies were wrapped in whatever the people died on, sheets or blankets, tied at both ends and were put in the mass grave."

At some point, the City of Victoria considered placing a school on the grounds of the old cemetery. At another time, the city thought to construct a picnic shelter on the site. Both ideas met with such protest that they were quickly abandoned.

"In view of recent requests for various uses of Memorial Square, may we, the Daughters of the Republic of Texas, renew our claim that Memorial Square remain as it is, a memorial cemetery," the Daughters wrote in a 1947 letter to the mayor and city council.

Mrs. C.F. Traylor also submitted a letter to the mayor in 1948 asking if it was true that the city was considering using the square "for purposes other than a cemetery."

"I am particularly interested in this property for the reason that it was dedicated many, many years ago as the last resting place for those pioneers who came to Victoria more than a hundred years ago," Traylor wrote, "and this spot is particularly dear and sacred to me because some of my people lie buried there."

One oddity sits above ground on Memorial Square: an ornate cement gatepost, with a historic monument, from the John J. Welder home, which used to take up the 700 block of Main Street. This was the home in which young Patti Welder died at the age of seventeen from typhoid fever in 1903.

A steam engine called the Old 771 was once displayed on the grounds that are adjacent to the old railroad depot, but the engine was removed to protect the solemnity of the spot.

"No place is more a part of our history than where we bury our dead," Wolff wrote.

Chapter 6

STREET OF TEN FRIENDS

The Street of Ten Friends, La Calle de los Diez Amigos, now Main Street, was intersected by streets named for friends of the fledgling colony of Victoria, founded in 1824 by Martin de Leon.

"The only names on the Street of Ten Friends that lived here were De Leon and [Rafael Antonio] Manchola. The others were military officers that may or may not have served with De Leon," Blanche de Leon said. "It is my impression they were intended to provide defense support for the colony when needed" against hostile Indigenous people.

The list includes the name of one military officer who would become an enemy to Victoria in later years.

Martin de Leon laid out his Mexican town according to age-old Spanish design. Street layout was mandated by Spanish colonial law, with streets gridded around a central plaza. He named the town for the patroness of Mexico, Our Lady of Guadalupe, now the patroness of the Americas. The name of the town was changed to Guadalupe Victoria later, perhaps by someone who processed De Leon's empresario contract in San Antonio. "Victoria" was likely tacked on as a nod to the first president of independent Mexico, Guadalupe Victoria. The president's birth name was Manuel Félix Fernández. He changed it to Guadalupe Victoria in honor of the patroness and Mexico's 1821 victory in its fight for independence.

Guadalupe Victoria's name appears as one of the ten friends on a historic marker designating the Street of Ten Friends near the intersection of East North and North Main Streets. The other names are Mateo Ahumada,

Captain Artiaga, Anastacio Bustamante, Rafael Chovel, Vincente Ramón Guerrero, Jose Manuel Rafael Simeon de Mier y Terán, De Leon, Manchola and Antonio Lopez de Santa Anna Pérez de Lebrón.

It may be hard for Texans to see Santa Anna as a friend of anyone's. "This, after all, is the man generations of Texas politicians have compared to every loathsome dictator from Adolf Hitler to Saddam Hussein, the Voldemort of Texas schoolchildren's nightmares, the great Mexican bogeyman," historians Bryan Burrough, Chris Tomlinson and Jason Stanford wrote in 2021.

But before Santa Anna became the Texas bogeyman, he was an intensely popular Mexican hero—and Victoria was a Mexican town. Santa Anna joined the Spanish colonial army in 1810 at the age of fifteen and gained rank as Mexico revolted against Spanish rule and later succumbed to political strife. He rose in power and popularity quickly and knew how to "smell the winds" of change, T.R. Fehrenbach wrote in *Fire & Blood: A History of Mexico*.

"Interestingly, his full name is Antonio de Padua María Severino López de Santa Anna y Pérez de Lebrón," University of Houston–Victoria research assistant Kevin Oliver said. He was named for St. Anthony of Padua, Oliver added. "And his father was a López, so it looks like his father was from 'Santa Anna,' a town in Spain. I don't know about Lebrón, from his mother's side; it was a popular surname in Andalucia."

"He speaks very friendly about Texas," Stephen F. Austin wrote about Santa Anna from Mexico City. "I am of the opinion that if you all keep quiet and obey the state laws that the substance of what Texas wants will be granted."

Santa Anna gave concessions to the Texians to avoid losing the northern province. He "withdrew government tax collectors from Texas for a year" and allowed Anglos to buy cheap land and make English a state language, among other concessions, Burrough, Tomlinson and Stanford noted. The Texians admired Santa Anna enough to consider themselves his followers, at one point.

In Mexico's civil strife, which pitted Centralists against Federalists, "the Texians declared themselves as allies of the federalist rebels [against a strong central power in Mexico City]. The federalists were known as santanistas, in honor of the general who initiated and led this revolt," Santa Anna, J.R. Edmondson wrote in *The Alamo Story*.

Of course, Santa Anna, with his nose to those winds of change, switched from the Federalist camp to the Centralist camp when the power in Mexico City was his. He stopped conceding and started suppressing, trying to keep Texas a part of Mexico and under Mexican law.

"We generally think of him only in the worst of ways and not without reason, considering what happened at Goliad and the Alamo," Henry Wolff Jr. wrote in a 1994 *Advocate* article.

Another name on the list of ten friends, Mier y Terán, would probably have told Santa Anna it was no use trying to hold on to Texas. He spent a year in Texas, heading a boundary commission and reporting on the state of the northern region.

As for Anglo-American Texans, "in things big and small, he found them obnoxiously independent-minded and quarrelsome, a people who 'go about with their constitution in their pockets,' ever alert to any infringement of their putative rights," Sam W. Haynes wrote in *Unsettled Land: From Revolution to Republic, the Struggle for Texas*. But Mexico was in a period of civil unrest, and Mier y Terán sensed his country would lose claim to Texas.

"How could Mexico expect to keep the lands above the Rio Grande 'when we cannot agree among ourselves?' he asked. 'The revolution is about to break forth, and Texas is lost,'" Haynes wrote. "The national humiliation was more than he could bear."

"En que parara Texas? En lo que Dios quiera (What is to become of Texas? Whatever God wills)," Mier y Terán wrote one evening.

The following morning, he "put on his full dress uniform and walked behind an abandoned church. Unsheathing his sword, he braced the handle against a stone and placed the tip against his heart, then plunged forward, impaling himself upon it," Haynes wrote. He had been a "dutiful public servant rather than an ambitious military chieftain," Haynes noted.

Four of the ten friends became Mexican presidents: Santa Anna, Guadalupe, Bustamante and Guerrero.

Fehrenbach noted that Guerrero was "down-to-earth," a man from a lowly station who rose to power in the Mexican military. He was a hero in the country's fight for independence from Spain.

Bustamente tried to stop American migration into Texas during his presidency, according to the Texas State Historical Association. He served as the fourth president and was president three times. Santa Anna was president eleven times.

Another man on the list of ten friends, Mateo Ahumada was the commandant of Texas in 1826, as noted in Ana Carolina Castillo Crimm's book *De Leon: A Tejano Family History*. He had correspondence with Manchola, a militia captain of La Bahia, who married one of Martin de Leon's daughters, Maria de Jesus, in 1824.

One of the final names on the list, Rafael Chovel, is more of a mystery. He appears as one of the colonists De Leon listed on his application for an empresario grant, but it is uncertain he whether lived in the colony. However, he is named as one of two Mexican officials to whom Mier y Terán's chronicler sent his report, according to an entry in the Yale University archives.

The final name is not even a name; it is a rank: Captain. Captain Artiaga is a mystery—that is, at least in Texas but perhaps not in Mexico. Certainly, Victoria's founder knew of him.

Chapter 7

VICTORIA'S FIRST CHRONICLER, VICTOR MARION ROSE

In the first forty-five years of Victoria's existence (1824–69), the townspeople resided under four successive national banners and experienced two wars and one enemy occupation.

In 1869, at the height of occupation by victorious federal forces after the American Civil War, Confederate cavalryman Victor Marion Rose returned from an Ohio prisoner-of-war camp and convalescence and took over management of the *Victoria Advocate*. Rose was a colorful character in the O'Connor lineage (by marriage) who would write the first complete history of Victoria, corresponding throughout the process with many original residents. His work, first titled *Some Historical Facts in Regard to the Settlement of Victoria, Texas*, is a priceless boon to anyone interested in the town's history.

Outside the Victoria County Courthouse, at 100 North Bridge Street, a historic marker celebrates Rose, who, the marker says, "left college to join the Confederate Army in the Civil War" and wrote much of the news sent home to Victoria during the war. The marker focuses mainly on the service of his writing both during and after the war.

One of Rose's descendants, a niece, Kate Stoner O'Connor, wrote a short biography of Rose for the 1961 edition of his history of Victoria, renamed *Victor Rose's History of Victoria*. The book is available at the Victoria Regional History Center.

After offering the dates of his birth and death—October 1, 1842, and February 5, 1893—O'Connor mentioned Rose's impressive lineage. "His father, John Washington Rose, was the son of William Pinckney Rose who commanded a company under General Andrew Jackson in the battle of New Orleans," O'Connor wrote. "William Pinckney Rose was the son of John Frederick Rose, a Revolutionary War sire who married Mary Washington, a niece of General George Washington."

O'Connor went on to mention twice in the following paragraphs that Rose "could hardly tell one horse from another" and relied on his friends to bring him his horse after parties lest he should ride off on someone else's mount.

He was, O'Connor wrote, "quite the ladies' man," writing love poems to woo his interests. "Once when he was about 14 years old, a beautiful young widow of about 30 years of age was visiting his mother," O'Connor wrote.

Victor Marion Rose. *Victoria Regional History Center.*

"She was quite a flirt and exercised her charms on the youth. Victor fell violently in love." When she left his mother's company, Rose followed her home, "where his father had to go and forcibly return him home." It would not be his last scandal involving a woman.

In 1859, Rose, then seventeen years old, shot and killed a man he believed was about to harm his brother, Volney, on a sidewalk in front of the Wheeler Store in Victoria. The murdered man's family sought justice, and so Rose's father, a representative of Victoria in the Texas Congress, spirited his son off to Louisiana. There, Rose attended college until the outbreak of the Civil War brought him home to enlist in the Confederate army in Victoria. He fought in many battles before he was taken prisoner and sent to Camp Chase, Ohio, O'Connor wrote.

"Here the brutal and inhuman treatment of the Confederate prisoners caused many deaths," O'Connor noted. "Rose came very near losing his life from starvation."

When he was released from the prison camp after the war, he traveled as far as Vicksburg, Mississippi, where he stayed with a family friend to recover his failing health. He returned to Victoria in December 1865. Yankee occupation troops were stationed at Forest Grove, the Rose plantation home, after the Civil War.

"Now on his return," wrote O'Connor, "he found the place desolate. The Negroes, demoralized, refused to work."

The family, unable to pay taxes on the land, lost their home. Rose's father died of tuberculosis in 1867. But Rose and other people tried to continue under occupation. "The young people improvised dancing parties in the country where there would be no disturbing elements in the blue coats," Rose wrote of the time after his return, "for the girls, bless their constancy and fidelity to a lost cause, could not be induced to dance with a Yankee."

He married early in 1866, but his young wife died in the 1867 yellow fever epidemic in Victoria. The couple had one daughter, Julia. Some years later, while Rose was working at the *Advocate*, a woman from South Carolina showed up on his doorstep, uninvited, claiming he had promised to marry her, O'Connor wrote. He refused her and "insisted that she leave, which she did, but leaving a pretty bad scandal behind her."

The scandal was such that Rose left Victoria and went to work for a newspaper in Laredo, where he published his history of Victoria and dedicated it to Colonel John J. Linn, one of his heroes from among the original Victoria colonists.

Chapter 8

THE "BLOODY HAND" OF A FEUD

After the American Civil War, for about ten years from 1865 to 1875, the counties of the Crossroads were covered in large part by what Victor Rose called "the bloody hand." Goliad County was especially drenched. Historian Henry Wolff Jr. called the years after the war "about the worst time in Texas" in a 1990 *Victoria Advocate* article. At the center of the mayhem was a war, of sorts, called the Taylor-Sutton Feud.

The Taylor gang were southern sympathizers, cattle thieves and murderers, by some accounts. Other accounts paint them as simple southern farmers, harassed by marauding Regulators. The Suttons and their kin were ranchers and lawmen, and they were considered Union men, even though William Sutton and others among them had fought for the Confederacy.

One among the Regulators, a captain among their numbers, was Jack Helm. of on the source of information, Helm was either a man bent on law and order and on delivering fugitives to justice or a vigilante and murderer out for personal gain. When captured men were shot and killed on the way to jail, the jargon of the day said they had been "Helmized," historian Chuck Parsons noted. Rewards could be collected for dead men as well as live ones.

"Jack Helm's story is a prime example of those law officers who operated on the fringes of the law" during Reconstruction (the period after the Civil War in the southern states), historian Kenneth W. Howell wrote in the introduction to Parsons's book *Captain Jack Helm: A Victim of Texas Reconstruction Violence*.

Regulators of Goliad County historic marker on the Courthouse Square in Goliad.

Two historic markers, one in Goliad County and one in Gonzales County, denote places important in Helm's story. The first marks the place he and his Regulators often operated, while the latter marks the place he was killed by Jim Taylor and the most notorious man in the Taylor gang, John Wesley Hardin.

Before Helm showed up on the scene at the Crossroads, he enlisted in the Ninth Texas Cavalry from his home in northern Texas. He deserted the Confederate army rather quickly. Speculation is that he deserted when he heard his fifteen-year-old bride, Minerva C. McCown, was having an affair, according to Parsons. He left the army and went home. She disappeared. "Minerva's fate remains a mystery," Parsons wrote.

Later, Helm was one among several locals, including his father, who hanged "five men sympathetic to the Union cause" in February 1862, Parsons noted. After the Civil War, these lawless executioners were being rounded up by Union troops, and so Helm left first for Austin and then for the Crossroads. There, he morphed into a seemingly devoted Union man and was at one time DeWitt County sheriff and at another time captain of the Regulators.

"The Regulators' work began in earnest in June 1869 in Goliad County where Sheriff Andrew Jackson Jacobs had requested help from the state due to the amount of lawlessness in his county," Parsons wrote.

The historic marker on the grounds of the Goliad County Courthouse, titled "Regulators of Goliad County," reads, "Gen. J.J. Reynolds, commander of the Federal forces, appointed Jack Helm special Marshal to the Goliad area in June 1868. A former deputy sheriff of DeWitt County, Helm captained a vigilante band of 50 men, mostly local ranchers, known as the Regulators." The marker goes on to say that the Regulators "pursued criminals with vigor and often with cruelty."

"Horse stealing and cow-skinning were getting to be dangerous occupations indeed," Parsons noted.

Helm started working with Captain C.S. Bell to hunt down two fugitives, Hays and Doboy Taylor, believed to have murdered Federal soldiers in Goliad County as well as a Federal officer in Mason, Texas.

The pair and an accomplice were at their father Creed Taylor's ranch in Karnes County during August 1869. Creed Taylor, notorious in later years, was a Texian soldier during the revolution and left a written account of that time, but in 1869, Bell described him as "the worst living man in this country." Bell caught up with the Taylors in Karnes County before Helm did. He killed Hays Taylor, wounded Doboy Taylor (who escaped) and arrested Creed Taylor, taking him to the county seat in Helena. Creed was jailed without any charges filed against him, mourning his son.

The feud became heated in Goliad County, the home of the Regulators.

"A correspondent identified only as 'Subscriber,' identified Helm's work—no doubt with tongue in cheek—writing that five or six men [in Goliad County] had 'suddenly taken off' but he knew not what caused their death or 'what particular ailment they had,'" Parsons wrote. Citizens were becoming uncomfortable with Helm's way of delivering justice, he noted.

Helm then sent a defense of himself to the *Victoria Advocate* in late August 1869, which was published in newspapers nationwide. It read, in part, "My men are kept under control, and no citizen can complain of the least injury at our hands. I labor for the supremacy of the law; without compensation or reward; and when the robbers are brought to justice, the

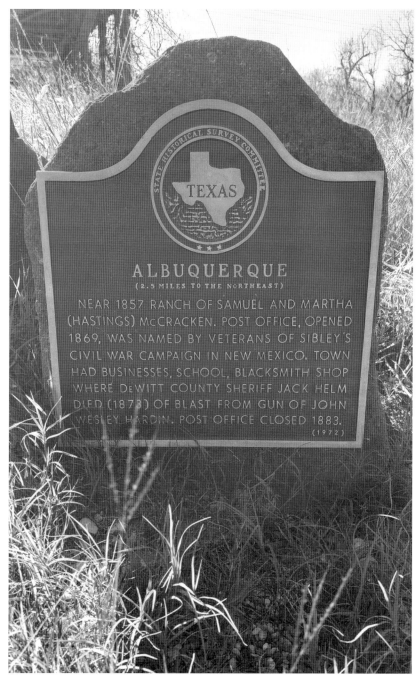

Albuquerque historic marker, noting where Captain Jack Helm was killed in DeWitt County.

majesty of the law vindicated—when honesty and industry can receive the fruits of their labors, I will be repaid for all."

The editor of the *Goliad Guard*, R.T. Davis, "had a high opinion of the man Helm, contrary to those who considered Helm the leader of a 'party,' which overpowered civil and military authorities," Parsons wrote. "Mr. Davis claimed that Helm's 'party' was 'composed of the best citizens of the county.'"

Despite this, bad blood was born between Helm and the Taylor gang.

The second historic marker is in Gonzales County, two and a half miles from where Helm was killed in DeWitt County at the town of Albuquerque. The place he was killed and his gravesite are located on private property. The town is long gone. The historic marker reads, in part, "Where DeWitt County Sheriff Jack Helm died (1873) of blast from gun of John Wesley Hardin."

Hardin did not act alone, however, and he may not have even fired the fatal shot. Contemporary accounts credit Jim Taylor with shooting the wounded Helm six times in the head.

Hardin's own account, written years later, reads, in part:

> *I looked around and saw Jack Helms* [sic] *advancing on Jim Taylor with a large knife in his hands. Someone yelled "Shoot the d----d scoundrel." It appeared to me that Helms was the scoundrel, so I grabbed my shot gun and fired at Capt. Jack Helms as he was closing in on Jim Taylor. In the meantime, Taylor had shot Helm repeatedly in the head, so thus died the leader of the vigilant committee, the sheriff of DeWitt, the terror of the county whose name was a horror to all law-abiding citizens.*

Other witnesses corroborated Hardin's story. So, was Helm lawful or lawless?

"It is not uncommon for Texas history and the mythology of the Old West to mingle, making it difficult to figure out just exactly what happened," Wolff once noted.

As for Victoria County, Victor Rose wrote in later years, "The 'Sutton-Taylor feud' and the Helm campaign did not affect Victoria County to any extent, as our citizens wisely refused to be drawn into the fearful vendetta. Fortunately, the bloody hand is now stayed."

Chapter 9

FIRST PEOPLES

West and north of San Antonio is the Balcones Escarpment, a fault line above which sits the Edwards Plateau—vast southern prairies and canyons, once teeming with bison and controlled by the Pehnahterkuh, the "Honey Eaters," the southernmost grouping of the fearsome Comanche.

These same Comanche, excellent horsemen once hunted in utter frustration by Juan Seguín, would lose all their chiefs in one fell swoop at a council meeting turned massacre in San Antonio on March 19, 1840.

Leaderless and in deep mourning, believing "bad medicine" had taken their chiefs, the people waited for a leader, a vision and good medicine. By August of the same year, a leader named Buffalo Hump had emerged, and the people prepared to set off on the war trail.

Avoiding the "bad medicine town," about six hundred to one thousand Comanche warriors and people passed north of San Antonio and headed toward Victoria and the coast, seeking revenge. About fifteen Victoria residents were surprised and killed by the raiding Comanche, while the town was mostly spared destruction. But Linnville, a port town on the coast established by Juan Linn and near present-day Port Lavaca, was less fortunate. The small town was destroyed. One woman taken captive survived because she wore a fashionable whalebone corset, which perplexed and thwarted the warriors.

Texans soon defeated the raiding Comanche warriors with the help of Tonkawa fighters, who later celebrated by roasting and eating the flesh of the defeated Honey Eaters.

NERMERNUH (THE TRUE HUMAN BEINGS)

The Comanche called themselves the True Human Beings, the Nermernuh. The name "Comanche" was applied to them in 1705 by a group of Utes who visited Spanish colonizers in New Mexico, Texas historian T.R. Fehrenbach noted.

"A small party of short, dark, squat Amerindians appeared in New Mexico, traveling with a band of mountain Utes," Fehrenbach wrote in his 1974 book *Comanches*. "The Spanish had never seen or identified either of these people. They were able to communicate with the Utes through other Indians, and the Utes described their companions as Koh-mahts, 'Those Who Are Always Against Us.'"

The name was later written as Comantz and eventually as Comanche, Fehrenbach wrote.

There was never a Comanche nation, in the European sense of the word. They numbered a "few thousand" spread across many bands of wanderers, Fehrenbach wrote. "No set of Europeans or Anglo-Americans ever came into contact with all of them at one time," he wrote.

Comanche children learned to ride as soon as they could mount a horse, and every Comanche was a skilled horseman. Once mounted, the people held Spanish expansion at bay and were eventually thought of as a "powerful barrier" against French and Anglo excursions into the northern province, Fehrenbach noted.

European settlers never understood Comanche culture, Fehrenbach wrote. To become civilized, in the Anglo sense, the Comanche would have to "betray his whole concept of the world and man's role in it, and destroy all of his cultural instincts and laws and beliefs—everything that to him seemed natural or sacred."

The horse warriors ruled Comancheria, a wide swath of land in Texas, New Mexico, Oklahoma, Nebraska and Colorado.

"Whether the stance was conscious or instinctive, the People had become a powerful barrier to all future movement across the plains," Fehrenbach wrote.

THE COUNCIL HOUSE FIGHT

During the winter of 1840, Colonel Henry Karnes, commander of the southern frontier region in the Republic of Texas, received three Comanche chiefs in San Antonio to discuss peace, historian Stephen L. Hardin wrote in a document titled "The Great Comanche Raid," on hand at the Victoria Regional History Center.

Karnes demanded that the Comanche release all their white captives before talks continued. The chiefs pledged to return with the captives.

On March 19, a Comanche chief named Maguara led sixty-five Comanche, including twelve chiefs and their women and children, into San Antonio for the council. To the Comanche, "a declared council was sacred," so Maguara and the other Comanche felt they had nothing to fear during talks, Fehrenbach noted.

"An impediment to negotiations became apparent," Hardin wrote. "The Indians had brought in only two captives, a small Mexican boy and the 15-year-old Matilda Lockhart. The girl's 'frightful condition' did nothing to improve Texian tempers."

A San Antonio woman who helped bathe and dress Matilda Lockhart described the girl's condition: "Her head, arms, and face were full of bruises, and sores, and her nose was actually burnt off to the bone. Both nostrils were wide open and denuded of flesh."

Inside the council house, on Alamo Plaza, the Texans demanded to know where the rest of the white captives were. The Comanche said they had none, while Lockhart said they had fifteen captives. The Comanche chiefs were informed they would be held hostage until the remaining white captives were brought to San Antonio. The chiefs refused to be taken and tried to fight their way out. They were all killed. The melee in the council house spread to the plaza, where the Comanche families were being observed by curious Bexarenos. The fight spilled onto the street and pitted these people against each other.

"Thirty chiefs and warriors, three Indian women, and three children lay dead," Hardin wrote. "Additionally, the Texians had captured and imprisoned 27 women and two elderly men." Eight Texans died in the fight.

One wife of a prominent chief was allowed to return to her people and "deliver the Texian demands for the release of all white captives." She arrived back in her camp wailing and mourning, Fehrenbach wrote.

"Braves swore vengeance for what they could only perceive as Texian perfidy and prepared for the greatest terror raid in the tribe's history," Hardin wrote. "Come Autumn they would thunder across white settlements like the icy wind that swept down from the Canadian River."

THE GREAT COMANCHE RAID:
VICTORIA AND LINNVILLE

"We in Victoria," John J. Linn wrote in *Reminiscences of Fifty Years in Texas*, "were startled by the sudden appearance of 600 mounted Comanches in the immediate outskirts of the village."

On August 6, Buffalo Hump's warriors attacked Victoria by complete surprise, "cutting down 15 people in the streets before they even realized they were under attack."

Many residents took refuge in Placido Benavides's roundhouse. "The building was in fact a Spanish-style torreon, the circular, tower-like, defensive turret, with toneras or gun slits on the lower floors, a style which the Spanish had learned from the Moors," Crimm wrote.

While Benavides had been exiled four years earlier and died in Louisiana in 1837, he still provided a refuge for the people of his family's colony.

"It just seems to me that back in 1840 in the little village of Victoria that Indians of that number would have been sufficient to make even the bravest youth evaporate on the spot," Henry Wolff Jr. wrote in a 1985 *Advocate* article, describing a group of schoolchildren who witnessed the raid.

The Comanche warriors broke off raiding Victoria the next day and headed down to the coast, where they looted and destroyed the port town of Linnville. When they first entered the town, they killed Major Hugh O. Watts, the collector of customs, Hardin wrote. They seized his wife, whom Fehrenbach described as a fair, handsome woman. They intended to take her as a captive and tried to strip her naked but fumbled with her whalebone corset. It was probably the first such garment they had encountered, Fehrenbach wrote. Becoming frustrated, they strapped Watts to a horse, dignity and undergarments intact.

Later, when being pursued by Texian Rangers, the Comanche killed all the captives. They tied Watts to a tree and fired a single arrow into her chest. They did not know, however, that her corset blunted the arrow's penetration and she survived.

They also chased a Victoria merchant named Wheeler, according to an eyewitness account by Gilbert Onderdonk. Wheeler had money stuffed into his hat, and as he spurred his horse ever faster, the hat and the money flew off his head.

The Comanche carried so much loot away from Linnville that it became an impediment, slowed their pace and resulted in battle at Plum Creek near present-day Lockhart. The Texians defeated the raiding Comanche, while some escaped back past the Balcones Escarpment. It was the last of the great Comanche raids.

Something of the Comanche has been romanticized in the legend of the American West. "For something in their lives—the hot thrill of the chase, the horses running in the wind, the lance and shield and war whoop brandished against man's fate, their defiance to the bitter end—will always pull at powerful blood memories buried in all of us," Fehrenbach concluded.

Chapter 10

EVERGREEN CEMETERY

I f Victoria's nearly two-hundred-year history was written into a high school textbook, Evergreen Cemetery could be a review for the final exam. The cemetery was the first community cemetery in Victoria and dates to 1850, Doris Gilpatrick and Becky Roell wrote in *The History and Heritage of Victoria County*, on hand at the Victoria Regional History Center. Located at the corner of Vine and Red River Streets, the cemetery holds the gravesites of many of Victoria's most famous inhabitants and storied individuals, as well as hundreds of lesser-known citizens.

Fifteen historic markers dot the landscape, including one at the entrance to the grounds that reads, "In 1849 John McCrabb bought 27 acres of a tract of land granted to the city by the Republic of Texas. The property already contained the gravesite of Dr. Walter Fosgate, who died in 1848. During the 1850s, part of McCrabb's land became the new public cemetery."

On the quiet fields, beneath stretching oak trees, rest the gravesites of Juan Linn and Victor Marion Rose, as well as William Sutton and Gabriel Slaughter.

A wrought-iron fence encloses the Historical Grave Shrine of the De Leon family in the oldest portion of the cemetery. While it is not known for certain that Martin de Leon is buried in Evergreen Cemetery, the shrine holds some of the members of his family. De Leon received land in the area after serving in the military for ten years, Crimm wrote in *De Leon: A Tejano Family History*. He had risen through the ranks to achieve a captaincy and received land as a reward, close to the year 1810.

Wrought-iron fence surrounding the De Leon grave shrine in Evergreen Cemetery.

"As part of acquiring the land, Martin carried out the formal act of possession. Accompanied by the government official granting the land, Martin was taken by the hand and 'pulled weeds and herbs from the earth in the name of his majesty the king and knelt in prayer giving thanks to God and the king,'" Crimm wrote.

De Leon captured and tamed wild mustangs on his ranch and raised cattle. Oftentimes, people traveling through would obtain horses from De Leon to ride for the remainder of their journey.

Noah Smithwick, Crimm wrote, was one such journeyman and left an account of De Leon and of Rancho Santa Margarita's horse wrangling. "Senor De Leon was the very essence of hospitality, as, indeed, I found the Mexicans everywhere to be," Smithwick wrote. However, seeing how the mustangs "reared and snorted," Smithwick and his companions "concluded walking would be a pleasant pastime compared to riding such steeds, so we continued our journey on foot."

Six De Leon family members have markers within the family shrine at Evergreen Cemetery. Each would have spent time on that first ranch, some as youngsters.

One of De Leon's first colonials, John Linn, known as Juan Linn, is buried not far from the De Leon shrine. A little way from Linn, his good friend Victor Marion Rose is buried. "Born in Victoria, Victor Marion Rose (1842–1893) left town for Laredo in the early 1880s,

Marker on the historical grave shrine of the De Leon family at Evergreen Cemetery.

with rumors of a scandalous love affair blazing at his heels," Henry Wolff Jr. wrote for a Texas Highways sidebar, on hand at the history center.

Rose, a historian, writer and editor, wrote a volume about the town's history titled *Some Historical Facts in Regard to the Settlement of Victoria*. A copy of the book was placed in the cornerstone of the Victoria County Courthouse in 1892, Wolff noted. It is also rumored that Rose ghostwrote Linn's memoir. The two books give a good account of the early years of the town.

Finally, off near a property fence, in a dark, old and seemingly almost forgotten portion of the cemetery near someone's backyard, a small obelisk reaches up toward the sky, marking the burial sites of William Sutton and Gabriel Slaughter. Sutton and Slaughter are tragic Old West figures straight out of the pages of the infamous Taylor-Sutton feud that consumed much of the Crossroads during the years following the American Civil War.

The Taylors were southern sympathizers and cattle rustlers, James Smallwood wrote in *The Feud That Wasn't*, a Texas A&M University Press publication. The Suttons were lawmen and ranchers, and arguably the most famous of their number was Deputy Sheriff William Sutton. The Taylors hatched a plan to murder Sutton as he and his pregnant wife were preparing to leave Texas on a passenger boat out of Indianola. Slaughter was supposed to be driving Sutton cattle up the Chisholm Trail at the time but did not feel well and so decided to accompany Sutton and his wife aboard the ship. As the men stood purchasing tickets for the trip, two Taylor gang members gunned them down in broad daylight.

"Sutton took several balls, including one to his back, one to his brain, another to his heart," Smallwood wrote. "As Laura Sutton began screaming, blood, gore, and brain matter seemed to have splattered everywhere, her dress included."

Slaughter had seen the Taylors and wanted to draw his pistol, but Sutton would not allow it, thinking they were safe on the busy waterfront. Instead of leaving Texas aboard a ship bound for New Orleans, the pair of dead men were carried to Evergreen Cemetery.

"Most early Victorians chose the town's Evergreen Cemetery as their final place of rest. Let's stroll among those chiseled stones and listen to a few of their stories," Wolff wrote.

Chapter 11

VICTORIA COUNTY COURTHOUSE AND AN INFAMOUS KILLER

The Victoria County Courthouse and America's first known serial killer are linked, albeit by a few degrees of separation.

The architect who designed the courthouse, built in 1892, also designed the Texas Pavilion for the 1893 World's Columbian Exposition in Chicago, as noted by historian Henry Wolff Jr. in a June 28, 1992 *Victoria Advocate* article. The exposition ran for six months and drew in over twenty-seven million visitors—and one killer who used the fair as a hunting ground.

The courthouse architect's name was James Riely Gordon, and the killer was Herman Webster Mudgett, also known as H.H. Holmes. Holmes is considered America's first known serial killer, and his gruesome crimes are documented in the book *The Devil in the White City*, by historian Erik Larson.

The White City was at the center of the exposition, designed by the top architects in the United States at the time. It was made incandescent with newfangled electric lights—thousands of glowing bulbs. Additionally, the technique of spray painting was invented to quickly paint the buildings, which were not permanent but made from materials easy to disassemble, like papier-mâché. "Each building was huge to begin with, but the impression of mass was amplified by the fact that all of the buildings were neoclassical in design," Larson wrote, "all had been painted the same soft white, and all were so shockingly, beautifully unlike anything the majority of visitors ever had seen in their own dusty towns."

On any day of the six-month-long exposition, hundreds of thousands of visitors arrived aboard trains from around the country.

The Victoria County Courthouse.

The Texas Pavilion designed by Gordon was not within the White City at the center but was still an impressive structure with twin towers and airy verandas, visited by hundreds of thousands of curious fairgoers.

Holmes recognized the potential to lure unsuspecting victims away from the copious crowds to his hotel down the road, without drawing attention to himself. He designed the hotel himself, before the exposition, with secret rooms, hidden passages and a torture dungeon, Larson wrote. He later admitted to killing at least twenty-seven people and was hanged to death. It's possible Holmes lured victims from the pavilion designed by Gordon.

Gordon, whose architectural firm was in San Antonio, won a statewide contest to gain the privilege of designing the Texas Pavilion for the exposition. He designed the pavilion while the Victoria County Courthouse was being built and while Holmes was designing and building his hotel, which would later be dubbed the "murder castle."

"At the age of 28 [in 1891], Gordon was chosen to design the Bexar County Courthouse," Wolff wrote, "and that launched a career that would

The Victoria County Courthouse, circa 1910. *Victoria Regional History Center*.

soon include such courthouses as the ones in Fayette and Victoria counties." Gordon, Wolff noted, is said to have designed over sixty courthouses around the United States.

The Victoria County Courthouse "is pretty much the way Gordon designed it—one of some 16 courthouses documented at the University of Texas Architecture Library as having been designed by Gordon in Texas, 12 of which are still standing," Wolff wrote.

Prior to Gordon's 1892 courthouse, Victoria had a less substantial building. In April 1846, a board of aldermen, including John Linn and J.O. Wheeler, "decided to build a 40-by-50 foot brick courthouse on what is the present day Courthouse Square," Tom E. Fite wrote in Roy Grimes's *300 Years in Victoria County*. The original courthouse was built in 1849.

"The small wood frame and plastered brick building was constructed by building contractor Richard Owens," according to a Victoria Preservation Inc. article. "It was a two story rectangular building with a wood cupola and two story wood porches typical of the prevailing vernacular Greek Revival style of the period."

It stood for fewer than fifty years. Later, the City of Victoria granted $64,487 to build the 1892 courthouse, Wolff noted. The even newer courthouse standing next to the historic Gordon building cost nearly $716,000 in 1967, by comparison.

"The Gordon courthouses rank among some of the more notable historic structures in Texas," Wolff wrote, "and it is a beautiful old building that still attracts considerable attention."

Gordon's career flourished, and he left Texas, setting up shop in New York City. He died in 1937.

As for Holmes, in a recent television documentary, one of his descendants claimed that Holmes was also Jack the Ripper. The infamous London killer was never identified.

Chapter 12

OTHER CHARACTERS FROM VICTORIA'S PAST

HILLER HOUSE

Most of the land that Riverside Park sits on once belonged to a German immigrant couple whose son fought for both the South and the North during the Civil War. The couple's home, dating from the late middle 1800s, still sits at the corner of Vine Street and Roseland Avenue. The Friedrich and Margaretha Hiller House is at the edge of the park with a historical marker calling it "the oldest extant structure of the historic Spring Creek Community." Friedrich and Margaretha Hiller immigrated to the United States in either 1851 (as on the marker) or 1852 (as in historic texts at the Victoria Regional History Center). They left Doettingen, Germany, and sailed to Galveston and then inland to Indianola, before settling in Victoria.

Many German families immigrated to America during this time, fleeing a failed democratic revolution in Europe. The revolutionaries were called Forty-Eighters, and many were wanted men in Europe. Much of the Texas Hill Country was settled by German Forty-Eighters who refused to support the Confederacy during the Civil War. Carl Schurz, a popular Union general, was a Forty-Eighter. He later became the United States secretary of the interior.

The Hillers brought with them a son, born in Germany in 1842. His name was Cristoph Hiller, known as Adam. Adam Hiller's obituary appeared in

Friedrich and Margaretha Hiller House.

the December 14, 1930 *Victoria Advocate* and explained his dual service during the Civil War. He was eighty-eight years old when he died.

"He was 19 at the outbreak of the Civil War and in July 1861 enlisted as a Confederate soldier, fighting with valor with the Southern forces in several important battles," the obituary said. He served in Victoria's Company B, Sixth Texas Infantry.

Hiller was captured at the Battle of Arkansas Post on January 11, 1863, and confined at a camp near Springfield, Illinois (Abraham Lincoln's hometown). "A month later he became a Union soldier by taking the oath of allegiance and received an honorable discharge at the close of the war after participating in many major engagements under Sherman," the *Advocate* reported.

Friedrich Hiller died of a severe cold on January 2, 1881, according to an article in *The History and Heritage of Victoria County*, compiled by the Victoria County Genealogical Society. Margaretha died one year later from an asthma attack.

The historic marker noted that Adam Hiller's brother Johann Michael moved into the home after the deaths, and the home became known for a while as the Mike Hiller House. Meanwhile, Adam Hiller married Victoria native Julia Schiwitz and fathered thirteen children.

No documentation at the Victoria Regional History Center told how Hiller was received upon returning home after changing sides during the Civil War. He lived the rest of his life peacefully in Victoria. One of the couple's sons, Johann Adam "Doc" Hiller, farmed the family land at Riverside Park. "He also hauled sand and gravel from the land near the present-day 14th green of Riverside Golf Course," reported the Genealogical Society.

The City of Victoria started buying Hiller land in 1935, according to the historic marker. The purchases continued until 1998.

On a final note: the Hiller land, surely worth a fortune today as Riverside Park, was valued at a mere $2,600 in 1870, according to census information in Roy Grimes's *300 Years in Victoria County*.

THE REGAN HOUSE

Personal diaries are a wonderful source of primary information about the past. Sometimes, the candid writing in a journal kept years ago speaks to the present about cringy things thought delightful decades ago.

Mary Virginia Hogan Regan kept a diary for three months in 1879, detailing her experience on "a little pleasure trip, business and pleasure combined," taken by her and her husband, Dominick H. Regan, through several states and a portion of Canada.

The couple's home at 507 South De Leon Street has a historic marker out front titled "Regan House." The Regan House was once located in the ill-fated town of Indianola. When that town was destroyed by a hurricane in 1886, the home held together, though it did float down the street a way before coming to rest against some sturdy cypress trees, according to one of the Regan children, Elleanore, who was along for the ride.

"What fun it was when her uncle and older brothers cut holes in the floor and the water came rushing up, along with miscellaneous cats, mice, and dogs, sweeping in on crests of the flood water," reported Victoria

The Regan House.

Preservation, Inc. from an interview with Elleanore. "When horses swam by and stuck their heads in the windows," she "squealed with delight and excitement."

Elleanore was young and did not understand the gravity of the situation, reported the preservation society.

After the devastating storm, Dominick Regan had the house disassembled and moved by rail to the less vulnerable city of Victoria. It was reassembled and has remained on De Leon Street since.

As the historic marker reads, "A fine example of Italianate Victorian design, the Regan house features jig-sawn porch detailing and polygonal bay windows."

Dominick Regan was born in Ireland in 1842 and came to America with his parents, John and Mary O'Regan, in 1852. The family settled in

New York, according to information found in the Weisiger Collection at the Victoria Regional History Center.

When the Civil War broke out in 1861, Regan enlisted in the Union army. The National Park Service Civil War Soldiers and Sailors Database lists just one Dominick H. Regan. He enlisted in the Union army in Illinois and served with the Eighty-Ninth Regiment, Illinois Infantry.

Regan's obituary in the October 11, 1927 *Victoria Advocate* reported that Regan served with General William Tecumseh Sherman's army in the western theater of war.

While carrying a satchel filled with mail, Regan was captured by two Confederate soldiers. They kept the mail and released Regan. After the war, he and his captors resided in the Victoria area and became fast friends. Those two captors were Colonel J.M. Brownson and Major William H. Kyle, according to Regan's obituary. Brownson was a pallbearer at the funeral of Regan's wife, who died shortly after giving birth to the couple's thirteenth child in December 1894, according to an article in *Historic Homes of Victoria, Texas*, published by Victoria Preservation, Inc.

Back now to the diary kept by Mary Regan. A transcription of the diary is on hand at the Victoria Regional History Center. Regan begins her travel diary on July 19, 1879, with the sentence, "Here we are starting off on a little pleasure trip, business and pleasure combined. I have left my darlings well and hope they will remain so."

Dominick (or Domenick, as his grandchildren spelled it in the preface to the diary) and Mary Regan were devout Catholics. Much of the diary, which covers a three-month journey, details the couple's visits to Catholic churches for Mass and vespers, as well as visits with church leadership.

At one point in the diary, the couple visits the Wisconsin Dells, and Mary splurges on the purchase of some postcards, much to Dominick's dismay. "Went to a gallery where they had lovely Photographic views of the Dells. I got a dozen & Domenick was not so very pleased at it," she wrote. "But they are beautiful & I know he will like them after we get home."

Mary seemed to love scenery, nature, flowers, ferns, church and the company of others all through her trip. But also in the pages of her diary are some brief entries that are offensive by present-day standards. For example, while in New York City, Mary mentions that she and Dominick went to a "Midgets palace & saw the tiniest human beings in the world. I could scarcely believe they were alive but saw it fully demonstrated before us they acted like any other children paid very little attention to the audience they talked, laughed sang & played with each other."

Mary Regan also uses the term "darkies" when referring to Black people in her diary, a common term in the late nineteenth century but discomforting to encounter now, even in the pages of a long-ago diary.

One final note: diaries are a clear, uncensored window into the past and one out of which viewers chance an encounter with the objectionable—for hidden in much of our past are things we know as shameful now that were not thought so then.

LORENZO DOW HEATON

Lorenzo Dow Heaton was a well-to-do businessperson. He owned a drugstore in Victoria and lived in one of the finest houses in town. As a hobby, Heaton examined mineral deposits along creeks and rivers in the Victoria area. He discovered oil before any major drilling in Texas got underway. He knew full well the value of his discovery, but he could not quite secure the backing of financiers to drill.

The Lorenzo Dow Heaton home stands at 307 South Bridge Street, across from the Victoria Police Department's downtown headquarters. A historical marker outside the Southern Colonial home pays homage to the native New Yorker who bought the home in 1875 and owned Heaton Bros. Pharmacy, once located on Main Street.

Sometime after 1875, Heaton, an amateur mineralogist, discovered oil in the Victoria area, according to Roy Grimes's *300 Years in Victoria County*.

"L.D. Heaton, a pioneer Victoria druggist and one of the city's more progressive citizens, who came from Potsdam, N.Y., had tried to interest Eastern capital in the oil and pottery prospects of this county, and at one time had the Chemical National Bank of New York in the notion of drilling here," Grimes wrote, "but something arose to interfere with those plans."

Oil was discovered in Texas in the 1860s, but the discovery was "modest," according to the American Oil & Gas

Heaton Bros. Pharmacy, circa 1890. *Victoria Regional History Center.*

104

Lorenzo Dow Heaton. *Victoria Regional History Center.*

Historical Society. "The first Texas oil boom arrived in June 1894 when the Corsicana oilfield was discovered by a drilling contractor hired by the city to find water," the society noted.

Victoria's brief foray into the oil business came about in a comparable manner, according to Grimes. "One of the first wildcatters [a prospector who sinks exploratory oil wells] appears to have been the City of Victoria itself, although the city did not intend to enter the oil business in 1909 when a contractor was hired to drill two artesian wells along the Guadalupe River," Grimes wrote in 1968.

The dig for the first water well proved promising for the discovery of oil, but it did not deliver. No oil was found, and Victoria dropped out of the oil business, Grimes wrote.

Heaton kept a jar of oil on display in his drugstore "that was said to have come from seep along Dry Creek a few miles southwest of the city." As it turned out, that was all the oil Heaton would ever claim.

Meanwhile, in 1889, two advancements made their debut in Victoria: citywide telephones were installed, and streetcars began operation. Streetcars, or street railways, were mule-drawn conveyances that ran on rails through downtown and the surrounding area. Heaton, whose drugstore had the new telephone number 49, was president of the board charged with creating the street railway in Victoria.

The November 11, 1889 *Advocate* reported:

> *It was difficult for spectators who gathered on the corner of Main and Constitution Streets on Monday afternoon to determine which was the most interesting, the beautiful car, the beautiful small mule or the handsome little driver. The trio brought [a] number to the corner, and a good load seated themselves in the car, but the mule was not inclined to proceed, he preferred to go the other way in crawfish fashion.*

The mule finally "got off alright," and the streetcar was a success.

Heaton also served as fire chief for the city near the turn of the century, when the fire department was a volunteer unit. It was considered a civic duty and an honor to serve as chief, Tom Tite wrote in Grimes's book. The chief was an elected official in a powerful position.

The department was "a potent force in local politics," Tite wrote, and was growing rapidly in the last years of the 1800s and early years of the 1900s— just a few decades removed from the use of leather bucket brigades.

In the spring of 1907, at the age of sixty-eight, Heaton died of "complications of diseases, which no medical skill could avert," his March 20 obituary in the *Advocate* reported.

"During the past 37 years Mr. Heaton had been one of our leading citizens," the *Advocate* reported. "He was perfectly honest and honorable in all his dealings."

It is certain Heaton lived during years of growth in Victoria and is ranked among the early businesspeople who nurtured important advances. All the while that jar of oil—that missed opportunity, perhaps—was exhibited in his store on Main Street.

GILBERT ONDERDONK

Without pioneer horticulturist Gilbert Onderdonk and his wife, Martha, founders of Nursery, fruit may not have been grown in Texas, especially not the variety of famous Texas peaches.

A historic marker at the north entrance to Nursery School, 13254 Nursery Drive, pays homage to Gilbert Onderdonk, the man credited with productive fruit farming techniques in Texas. His wife, Martha, purchased one hundred acres near the new Victoria-Cuero Railroad line in 1883 for a branch of the Mission Valley Onderdonk Nursery.

"A post office named Nursery soon opened," the marker reads, "and Gilbert Onderdonk served as both postmaster and Wells Fargo shipping agent. The small town of Nursery grew up around the railroad, post office and nursery operations."

Evelyn Oppenheimer penned a University of North Texas Press study of Onderdonk in 1991, titled *Gilbert Onderdonk: The Nurseryman of Mission Valley, Pioneer Horticulturist*. A horticulturist is an expert in garden cultivation and management, according to the Oxford English Dictionary. Oppenheimer gives Onderdonk credit for developing fruit farming in Texas.

"It was Gilbert Onderdonk who began and developed production of fruit in Texas," Oppenheimer noted. "Onderdonk literally planted the foundation of the vast production of Texas fruit today."

Before Onderdonk's successful nursery, it was believed that fruit could not be grown in this section of Texas, the Texas State Historical Association wrote. "His success dispelled the previously accepted notion that fruit could not be grown in that part of Texas. He originated or introduced into Texas more than seven peach varieties, at least eleven plum varieties, as well as the Victoria mulberry and the Lincoln apple," Oppenheimer and Craig Roell wrote for a historical association article.

Onderdonk "collected and raised specimens of fruits and flowers and furnished the area between the Rio Grande and New Orleans with acclimated fruit trees and shrubs," Oppenheimer wrote.

Onderdonk was a Dutch native New Yorker who traveled to South Texas in 1851 in search of a warmer climate, hoping to ease his fragile health. His health quickly improved, and he taught school and worked on a local ranch. He eventually raised his own horses, until 1856, when he sold his herd for a profit, Oppenheimer wrote. He married Martha and bought 360 acres in Mission Valley and began his nursery operations there in about 1858. He quickly gained renown as a nurseryman, publishing news extensively about his work, Oppenheimer said. He served in the Confederate army during the Civil War, was taken prisoner and later returned home.

As Oppenheimer put it, by the time of Onderdonk's death in 1920 at the robust age of ninety-one, he had been a pioneer botanist and horticulturist, a rancher, a Confederate soldier, a traveler throughout Mexico for the U.S. Department of Agriculture, a prolific letter writer and essayist, a travel writer for newspapers and a man of family, property, international recognition and fame among horticultural experts in Europe for his work in South Texas.

An *Advocate* article published upon his death on September 9, 1920, titled "Tribute to the Memory of a Horticulturist," agreed with Oppenheimer's assessment of Onderdonk. "There are a great many men throughout our country who have blazed the trail and made civilization possible," the article said. "Many of these pioneers have left legacies of experience and knowledge to future generations. One of these was Gilbert Onderdonk."

THE HAUSCHILD OPERA HOUSE

Many years ago, Victoria was home to a wildly popular casino, but no one went there to gamble. That casino eventually gave way to an opera house, equally as popular, but no one went there to hear intense Italian dramas belted out in tenors and sopranos.

Casino Hall was the center of social activity in Victoria until the Hauschild Opera House opened in 1894.

A historic marker is affixed to the building that was once home to the opera house at 202 East Forrest Street in downtown Victoria. Casino Hall is long since gone. At the time of Casino Hall's prominence in Victoria, from about 1854 through 1893, casinos were not gambling facilities but rather social gathering spaces with a ballroom being the main attraction.

Casino Hall was forty feet wide and ninety to one hundred feet long. The first floor housed a ballroom, bar and stage, according to historic documents at the Victoria Regional History Center. Popular bands and traveling theater groups performed at the casino, which was located on Bridge Street.

"In 1893 the late G.H. Hauschild built Hauschild's Opera House, sounding the death note for Casino Hall," a history center article noted. "The old building was purchased by Charles DeWitt, who built three homes from its Florida lumber."

On March 26, 1894, the opera house opened. It was a Monday evening, and the Charles Walthen Chase Company performed a play titled *Uncle's Darling*, a comedy.

"The audience that assembled in Hauschild's Opera House were enraptured with the beauty of their surroundings," the *Advocate* reported, "and the expressions of admiration were numerous indeed. Several ladies were heard to remark that it was worth the price of admission to gaze on the stage curtains and draperies."

The cost to attend the opera house depended on the popularity of the play. It could cost anywhere from twenty-five cents to two dollars per ticket.

"People would come into town from miles around by horse and buggy to catch a show at Hauschild's Opera House," an August 23, 1974 article in the *Advocate* reported.

It cost George Hermann Hauschild $25,000 to erect the building, and it was considered "the showplace of the day for Victoria."

"There are larger opera houses in the state, but this is large enough," the *Advocate* noted. "It's [*sic*] seating capacity is about 800."

The same article mentioned that the chairs "were purchased from the Grand Rapids [Michigan] School Furniture Company" and "the scenery is from Sosman and Landis' great scene painting studio of Chicago." The lighting fixtures, including a large ornate chandelier, were also purchased from a company based in Chicago.

Hauschild and his wife, Adele Luder Hauschild, moved to Victoria in 1866. The couple met during the Civil War in New Orleans, where Hauschild was a "second Lieutenant in the Confederate Army's Hansa Guards regiment defending the city," an April 21, 1986 *Advocate* article reported.

Hauschild opened a hotel, the Hermann House, in Victoria in 1867, boasting "a stable always supplied with fresh provender [that] is attached to the premises."

An undated report in the *Advocate*, on hand in a Hauschild file at the history center, mentioned that "sneak thieves entered the Hermann House, on Forrest Street, and helped themselves to considerable bed clothing, stripping two beds. This is partly chargeable to the cold snap."

Hauschild opened four businesses in Victoria, including the Hermann House and Hauschild Opera House. He served on the school board for twenty years and was the city alderman for fourteen. He and his wife had seven children, three daughters and four sons. Their eldest daughter, Julia, was a popular Victoria socialite, even inspiring Canadian composer Frederick Abbott to write a song about her titled "The Sweetest Girl in All the State of Texas." Julia and her younger sister, Adele, also belonged to a local young women's shirtwaist club in 1898. The club's motto was "We won't get married—'til we're asked."

Hauschild's eldest son, George Henry, managed a music store on the lower level of the opera house. The music store was in business until 1980, but the opera house closed during the 1930s, unable to compete with the newfangled motion pictures, or "talkies," as they were then known.

"Hauschild's Opera House then became a 'mausoleum of ghosts,'" an *Advocate* reporter wrote in the 1950s.

PROFESSOR O.E.H. MUNDT

Professor O.E.H. Mundt presided over a successful public school on Glass Street for eleven years, but the man is a bit of a mystery. A thorough search of sources at the Victoria Regional History Center offered nothing complete about Mundt, but an interesting picture formed from the scraps.

Mundt came to Victoria in 1893, opened a popular school before there was a school district, helped kill off local prairie chickens, was president of the Casino Society and was once charged with and found innocent of using "abusive language" during a fight on Main Street in 1898.

He had five children, and in 1898, his three young sons, all apparently under ten years old at the time, tried to convince him to allow them to enlist as messengers on navy ships headed to the Spanish-American War.

A historic marker affixed to Mundt Place at 103 Glass Street notes that the building, once the Continental Hotel, served as Mundt's school from 1893 until 1904. The Continental Hotel was built in 1871 and owned by a county judge named R.H. Coleman. Coleman was once charged with assaulting a waiter in his establishment.

"Irritated by what seemed to be systematic negligence on the part of the waiter, the accused threw a glass at the [waiter] and then chased him around the room with a six shooter," the *Victoria Advocate* reported. He was not convicted of the assault, but the grand jury "also returned three other indictments against Judge Coleman for the unlawful carrying of a pistol."

The Continental Hotel boasted "the coolest rooms of any house in Victoria" in an 1884 advertisement in the *Advocate*. By 1893, those cool rooms had become schoolrooms operated by Mundt.

"With the coming of Prof. Mundt to Victoria in 1893 another public school was begun," the *Advocate* reported in 1928. "The enrollment was near 400 pupils." A small tuition was paid to attend.

Once the Victoria Independent School District was established in 1898, school was free for students from first through seventh grade, but those in grades eight through ten paid $2.50 a month, according to a 1968 *Advocate* article. Taxes were soon implemented to cover the cost of education, and tuition was dropped.

On July 5, 1904, Mundt received a message from Houston informing him that he had been elected principal of the public schools there.

Mundt was born in Germany in 1855 and married there before coming to Texas. He died of heart failure in 1911, when he was fifty-five years old. His time in Victoria spanned just over a decade, it seems, but he left behind a couple of stories that made it into the town's historic record.

An 1897 *Advocate* article mentioned that Mundt and a couple of friends "started out before daylight this morning to lessen the number of prairie chickens in some quarter of the country." The wild chickens were eventually eradicated in the area.

Mundt was president of the Casino Society when Casino Hall was offered for sale in 1900, making him the final president.

On April 7, 1898, Mundt engaged in a street brawl, according to an *Advocate* report that is worth reading in its entirety: "A difficulty occurred last night on Main Street, between O.E.H. Mundt and Chas Lawrence. We have not been able to learn the particulars, but it seems for some reason Mr. Mundt shook his fist in Mr. Lawrence's face and the latter struck him. Friends interfered and the combatants were separated." Mundt was charged with using abusive language but was found not guilty a year later.

Mundt had five children, two girls and three boys. One daughter, Otelia, became ill after he left for Houston. Mundt had moved there without his family, who remained in Victoria. The nine-year-old girl was sick for several weeks. Mundt returned to see her before she died on February 9, 1905.

In 1898, the *Advocate* printed a short article titled "Wanted to Go to War," relating a story about Mundt's three young sons. Mundt, it said, "informed the oldest of the three the other day that Uncle Sam had decided to use boys as messengers on board ships and asked him if he would be willing to go. 'You bet I would,' ejaculated the boy."

The boy informed his brothers, who then asked to go as well. "Finding that his boys were really in earnest, Mr. Mundt had to tell them better," the article concluded. They would not go to war.

Only one of his children, a son, remained in Victoria at the time of his death. The others lived in El Paso. What became of the school and the building after Mundt left is unclear. In 1946, it was purchased from the Mundt family by Post 4146, Veterans of Foreign Wars, according to the historic marker.

The building stands empty. The blinds in the windows are yellowing and damaged. One step on the front porch is missing. There is a smell of age and mold. But it stands 157 years after it was built.

Chapter 13

A TRAGIC EVENT
SOUTH OF VICTORIA

On a mid-May day in 1902, a massive tornado tore across the San Antonio River near Goliad. "The water of the river was sucked up into the clouds, so that the river was dry," according to one witness.

The cyclone then roared into Goliad within mere moments, killing 114 people, including 50 churchgoers attending Sunday service at a Black Methodist church. All 50 were crushed and instantly killed. They are buried in a mass grave on the eastern edge of Lott Cemetery, a Black cemetery outside Goliad, on Sunrise Road. A simple marker—"In Remembrance of the May 18, 1902, Tornado Victims"—marks the burial site.

Henry Wolff Jr., writing for the *Victoria Advocate* in an article marking the one-hundred-year anniversary of the 1902 tornado, recorded, "There are conflicting reports as to how many were buried in the mass grave, one account indicating '34 victims plus one leg.'"

The F4 tornado, listed as the second most deadly in Texas's history by the National Weather Service, killed 114 people in Goliad and injured over 200 more.

A historic marker designating the remarkable storm rests on Goliad's Courthouse Square. The marker leads the reader to another outside the Fannin Street United Methodist Church, a few blocks away, on the corner of Mount Auburn and Fannin Streets. Finally, the curious can follow through to the marker at Lott Cemetery.

Immediately after the tornado, no one was certain how many people had been killed. The day after the tornado, May 19, 1902, the *Victoria Advocate*

Above: Goliad Tornado of 1902 historic marker on Goliad's courthouse square.

Left: Historic marker indicating where the Black victims of the 1902 tornado were buried in a mass grave in Goliad's Lott Cemetery.

Historic marker at Lott Cemetery in Goliad.

reported on the killer storm in an article titled "Terrific Cyclone at Goliad: Death and Destruction in Its Wake—132 People Dead Many Wounded—Victoria Sends Aid."

"Yesterday afternoon, at about 4 o'clock the appalling news was flashed over the wires: 'Terrible Cyclone at Goliad,'" reported the *Advocate*. "The intelligence quickly spread over the city, causing general consternation and apprehension for the safety of relatives and friends. Soon followed an appeal for help from the stricken town."

In the text of *The History and Heritage of Goliad County*, on hand at the Victoria Regional History Center, the Goliad Historical Commission compiled a few eyewitness accounts from that terrible May day. It includes the story of a farmer named Mr. Johnson, who had made several cattle drives to Kansas during the golden age of the Chisholm Trail. The storm was brewing, and Johnson "looked up from his barnyard chores, then studied the clouds." He noticed black cones reaching down from the dark sky "into long, twisting streamers." The story continues with Johnson's account of what he said upon seeing the angry sky: "Them things keep acomin' down and keep on acomin' thisaway," he remarked, "somebody 'round here's gonna get plumb blowed away."

Another storm survivor, Kate Chilton Talbot, was just ten years old when the twister struck. "I was taken up into the air for a few minutes. I just remember rolling in the water when I came down," she recalled. She had a scar on her head from an injury she'd suffered on her wild ride.

Wolff's personal research file about the 1902 cyclone is also on hand at the regional history center. It contains a remarkable letter sent to Wolff by a Victoria resident with roots in Goliad. The man related what his father and grandfather recalled about the storm.

His grandfather had owned slaves who were emancipated by General Gordon Granger's June 19, 1965 General Order No. 3, proclaiming the end of legalized slavery in Texas. This is the origin story of the holiday now celebrated as Juneteenth. The man wrote that the freeing of the slaves upset his grandfather. Three of the slaves decided to stay with him. One, he said, was a big man with exceptionally large feet. He had gone into town the day the tornado struck. (The tornado hit thirty-six years after slavery ended.)

His father and grandfather grew concerned after the storm and went to search for the former slave. They found him dead and were able to identify him only by his large feet, the man wrote to Wolff. He did not name the former slave. Many of the people killed in the Fannin Street church were former slaves as well, according to historic documents.

When the dead were first listed, as recorded in documents at the history center, each white person killed was listed on a single line with a title, such as Mr. or Mrs. or "mother of." They were listed separately with any of their children who were killed. The list of African Americans killed was a block of names, one after the other, no designations of any sort. Mexican Americans killed were not named, only numbered.

One final note: at the Lott Cemetery there is a gravestone with a single word etched into it: "Bingo." Bingo was an orphaned Black boy raised by "prominent cattleman Ed Lott's wife. He died around 1916," according to the historical marker at the cemetery.

Conversation with history often brings with it uncomfortable talking points. The 1902 Goliad tornado is no exception. It brings segregated cemeteries, slavery and numbered and unnamed Mexican American victims into the story.

"History is, to say the least, complicated," historian and Texas native Annette Gordon-Reed wrote in her book *On Juneteenth*.

Chapter 14

A MODERN BUSINESSPERSON, A HISTORIC BUSINESS

N ancy Garner is not very interesting, or so she says. Her modesty is sincere, but one look around her office at Woolson Realty begs the question, "How so?"

One wall is bedecked with big-game hunting photos. Garner and her husband, children and grandchildren smile from the photos in the collage, sometimes dwarfed by their quarry. On the floor in front of the photos is a display with impressive elk and mule deer trophies.

On another wall, an American flag is encased in glass with a certificate denoting where it had flown, including on the USS *Enterprise* when Garner landed aboard the aircraft carrier while it was floating in the Bermuda Triangle.

Behind Garner's desk, on the wall facing visitors, is a large, colorful painting of a cow, and that is where her story began. She was born in San Angelo, in West Texas, but has lived in Victoria since the early 1980s, she said. She spent her childhood on a ranch, sometimes traveling with her family to Wyoming, Colorado and Montana to sell livestock. She said the trips were not for fun but rather strictly for business.

"My dad was a livestock commission buyer, so he bought and sold livestock like I do real estate," Garner said on October 20, 2023. "People would call him to see if he could find them, for example, a thousand head of sheep. He would then get the livestock and bring them in, and we would work them." She said the family raised sheep and cattle and often hunted for meat.

She attended Lakeview High School in San Angelo and then moved east to Victoria, where she attended night school at Victoria College and the University of Houston–Victoria.

"I sort of took a long way around because I went to night school," Garner said. "I got an associate degree from Victoria College, and then I took classes to pass the CPA [certified public accountant] exam. I was working and had a child, so it took a while, but I got enough hours in to pass the CPA."

She passed the exam in 1989, she said, and purchased Woolson Real Estate in 1996. She worked for Woolson for years before that.

Her hard work and dedication to the business paid off. She worked closely with the business's original owner, Robert Bruce Woolson, for more than a dozen years before she assumed the reins. Woolson started the business in 1964.

He was "born on June 26, 1920, in Detroit, Michigan to the late Robert B. and Elizabeth Gunn Woolson. He graduated from high school in 1939 from Morgan Park Military Academy in Chicago, Illinois and attended college at the Citadel Military College in Charleston, South Carolina until he enlisted in the U.S. Air Force in 1941," Woolson's obituary in the *Advocate* noted.

"Almost any older resident in Victoria will know of Robert Woolson," Garner said with a smile. "He was quite a gentleman. He was a lieutenant colonel in the Air Force. He flew missions on D-Day. He was a very interesting man."

Woolson "had the honor of flying 35 combat missions during World War II as a B-24 co-pilot, including two on D-Day," his obituary noted.

Garner said when she bought the company that she kept Woolson's name "partially out of respect, and it was one of the oldest companies." The name was recognized by people in town.

Woolson died on September 17, 2012, at the age of ninety-two, about sixteen years after Garner bought the company.

Garner expressed a dedication to Woolson's legacy and to Victoria. Her favorite projects are those that restore old structures, bringing new life and new business to her adopted town.

Woolson Real Estate manages the tallest building in town, One O'Connor Plaza. She manages multiple apartment complexes around town as well.

"One of the things I have been kind of proud of is seeing the old Victoria Advocate building coming to life. I sold the building to the county, and now it is the Victoria Regional Disaster Response and Recovery Center," Garner said.

She was also involved in the sale of the building that houses the Gulf Bend Center, she said. "I was asked to work with that building. It was called

Victoria Regional Medical Center back then," Garner said. "It was a big empty building. So, I went to Gulf Bend and talked with the executive director. We put the deal together, and that building is thriving now. They work with all kinds of people suffering with mental health disorders and addictions."

"I love those kinds of transactions where you take a building that is toward the end of its life or single purpose and find that next purpose for it," Garner said. "Those are things that I am extremely proud of. I sold Mitchell School for the school district last year."

The Mitchell School, originally opened as a high school in 1902, is now the Mitchell Artisan Market & More. The shopping spot opened recently and houses Bark n' Blooms, a build-your-own dried flower bar, and the Sip and Shine Café, among other businesses.

Garner is president of two apartment complexes she said she planned and built, The Whittington and Reserve Apartment homes.

She stays busy, she said, and has no plans yet to retire. Once a year, in autumn, Garner goes to northern New Mexico to hunt elk and mule deer. She recently broke her hand and will have surgery to repair the damage but said she still plans to make the annual trip after the surgery. She hunts in the mountains of New Mexico, sometimes at an elevation of eleven thousand feet, in Raton, just south of the border with Colorado.

Hunting is a common activity for her and her family. When not in New Mexico, they hunt white-tailed deer and hogs closer to home. She taught her son, stepson and grandchildren gun safety, as well as to dress out what they kill.

While hunting is a norm for Garner, landing on the USS *Enterprise* was a once-in-a-lifetime sort of feat. She was young when the movie *Top Gun* was a hit, and she said she became enamored with the aircraft carrier imagery. "I got to be catapulted off of an aircraft carrier," Garner said. "I was just fortunate."

She said she wanted to know what it felt like to take off from one, and take off she did. "I wrote the right letters" to the right people, Garner said, and was granted permission to fly out to the USS *Enterprise*.

In 1998, she was flown from Norfolk, Virginia, with a few other civilians, out to sea. In the Bermuda Triangle, the group landed on the deck of the USS *Enterprise*. The *Enterprise* was the first nuclear-powered aircraft carrier and the eighth United States naval vessel to bear that name. The carrier was 1,123 feet long and served for fifty-five years, being decommissioned in 2017.

"It was just exhilarating. It was amazing. I didn't think as much about landing as taking off, but it was equally jarring," Gardner said. "I was the only lady on board, and I just got to see everything."

The encased flag in her office includes a certificate that says the flag flew over the USS *Enterprise* while Garner was aboard on February 20, 1998, at "Latitude 36 degrees 50 Minutes Longitude 76 degrees 07 Minutes."

The flag was also flown over the USS *Lexington* at Corpus Christi, as well as over the Chief of Naval Air Training. Now, it is proudly displayed by Garner—a remarkably interesting Victoria businessperson, owner of a historic real estate company, with quite a story of her own.

BIBLIOGRAPHY

Newspapers

Houston Telegraph
Victoria Advocate

Periodicals

Discover 361

Books and Articles

Acosta, Teresa Palomo, and Ruthe Winegarten. *Las Tejanas: 300 Years of History*. Austin: University of Texas Press, 2003.

"Across Opera House Stage: Parade of Celebrities." *Victoria Advocate*, August 23, 1974.

Bonekemper, Edward H., III. *The Myth of the Lost Cause: Why the South Fought the Civil War and Why the North Won*. UK: Regency History, 2015.

Boyd, Bob. *The Texas Revolution: A Day-by-Day Account*. San Angelo, TX: San Angelo Standard, 1986.

Burrough, Bryan, Chris Tomlinson and Jason Stanford. *Forget the Alamo*. New York: Penguin Books, 2021.

Campbell, Randolph B. *An Empire for Slavery: The Peculiar Institution in Texas, 1821–1865*. Louisiana paperback edition, 1991. Baton Rouge: Louisiana State University Press, 1989.

Crimm, Ana Carolina Castillo. *De Leon: A Tejano Family History*. 1st ed. Austin: University of Texas Press, 2003.

Edmondson, J.R. *The Alamo Story: From Early History to Current Conflicts*. 2nd ed. Helena, MT: Two Dot, 2022.

Fannin, James Walker, Jr. James Walker Fannin Jr. to Joseph Mims, February 28, 1836. In *Reminiscences of Fifty Years in Texas*, by John J. Linn. New York: D. & J. Sadlier & Co., 1883.

Fehrenbach, T.R. *Comanches: The History of a People*. New York: Anchor Books, 2003.

———. *Fire & Blood: A History of Mexico*. New York: Macmillan Publishing, 1973.

Frazier, Donald S. *Fire in the Cane Field: The Invasion of Louisiana and Texas, January 1861–January 1863*. Kerrville, TX: State House Press, 2009.

Gordon-Reed, Annette. *On Juneteenth*. 1st ed. New York: Liveright Publishing Corporation, 2021.

Grimes, Roy, ed. *300 Years in Victoria County*. Victoria, TX: Roy Grimes and the Victoria Advocate Publishing Co., 1968.

Hammett, A.B.J. *The Empresario Don Martin de Leon*. Waco, TX: Texian Press, 1973.

Hardin, Stephen L. *Texian Iliad: A Military History of the Texas Revolution*. Austin: University of Texas Press, 1994.

Harrigan, Stephen. *Big Wonderful Thing: A History of Texas*. Austin: University of Texas Press, 2019.

Harsdorff, Linda. "Innkeeper Made Entertainment Mark: The Hauschild Opera House Was a Showplace When It Opened in 1894." *Victoria Advocate*, April 21, 1986.

Hauschild, Henry J. *A Musical Chronicle from the Historical Scrapbooks of Henry J. Hauschild*. Austin: Whitley Co., 1999.

Haynes, Sam W. *Unsettled Land: From Revolution to Republic. The Struggle for Texas*. 1st ed. New York: Basic Books, 2022.

John, Linn J. *Reminiscences of Fifty Years in Texas*. Kerrville, TX: State House Press, 1986.

Larson, Erik. *The Devil in the White City: Murder, Magic, and Madness at the Fair That Changed America*. New York: Vintage Books, 2003.

Matovina, Timothy M. *The Alamo Remembered: Tejano Accounts and Perspectives*. Austin: University of Texas Press, 1995.

Montejano, David. *Anglos and Texans in the Making of Texas, 1836–1986*. Austin: University of Texas Press, 1987.

Olmsted, Frederick Law. *A Journey through Texas, or a Saddle Trip on the Southwest Frontier*. Lincoln: University of Nebraska Press, 2004.

Oppenheimer, Evelyn. *Gilbert Onderdonk: The Nursery Man of Mission Valley, Pioneer Horticulturalist*. Denton: University of North Texas Press, 1991.

Parsons, Chuck. *Captain Jack Helm: A Victim of Texas Reconstruction Violence*. Denton: University of North Texas Press, 2018.

Petty, J.W., Jr., ed. *A Republishing of the Book Most Often Known as Victor Rose's History of Victoria*. Victoria, TX: Book Mart, 1961.

Pruett, Jackie L., and Everett B. Cole. *The History and Heritage of Goliad County: Researched and Compiled by Goliad County Historical Commission*. Goliad, TX: Goliad Historical Commission, 1983.

Regan, Mary Virginia Hogan. *Diary: July 18, 1879–September 8, 1879*. Victoria, TX: Victoria Regional History Center, Special Collections.

Rose, Victor M. *Some Historical Facts in Regard to the Settlement of Victoria, Texas: Its Progress and Present Status*. Laredo, TX: Daily Times Print, 1883.

Scheer, Mary L., ed. *Women and the Texas Revolution*. Denton: University of North Texas Press, 2012.

Smallwood, James. *The Feud That Wasn't: The Taylor Ring, Bill Sutton, John Wesley Hardin, and Violence in Texas*. College Station: Texas A&M University Press, 2008.

Spurlin, Charles D., ed. *Civil War Diary of Charles A. Leuschner*. 1st ed. Austin: Nortex Press, 1992. From collection at the Victoria Regional History Center.

"Terrific Cyclone at Goliad." *Victoria Advocate*, May 8, 1902.

Tijerina, Andrés. *Tejano Empire: Life on South Texas Ranchos*. College Station: Texas A&M University Press, 1998.

TSHA. Your Texas. Your History. www.tshaonline.org/home.

Urbano, David. *The Saga of a Revolutionary Family: The Martin De Leon Family of Texas*. San Antonio: University of Texas, 1990.

Victoria County Genealogical Society. *The History and Heritage of Victoria County*. Vol. 1. Victoria, 2000.

———. *The History and Heritage of Victoria County*. Vol. 2. Victoria, 2000.

———. *The History and Heritage of Victoria County*. Vol. 3. Victoria, 2003.

Wolff, Henry, Jr. "Bad Time for Texas." *Victoria Advocate*, October 4, 1990.

———. "Courthouse Designer a Busy Man." *Victoria Advocate*, June 28, 1992.

———. "Frontier Life Hard." *Victoria Advocate*, February 24, 1983.

———. *Henry's Journal: Historically Speaking*. Victoria, TX: Victoria Advocate Publishing Co., 1999.

———. "The Indian Raid." *Victoria Advocate*, August 8, 1985.

———. "John Wright Wrong Man for 'Mother of Texas.'" *Victoria Advocate*, September 5, 1999.

———. "1902 Goliad Cyclone Did Some Strange Things." *Victoria Advocate*, May 17, 2002.

———. "Raid Helped End Linnville." *Victoria Advocate*, February 10, 1999.

———. "Two Historical Ladies." *Victoria Advocate*, May 4, 1984.

———. "Victoria Had Some Mayhem during Reconstruction." *Victoria Advocate*, August 31, 2008.

Zamora, Emilio, Cynthia Orozco and Rodolpho Rocha, eds. *Mexican Americans in Texas History*. Austin: Texas State Historical Association, 2000.

ABOUT THE AUTHOR

Tamara Joy Diaz is a Global Honors graduate of the University of Washington–Tacoma, with a major degree in American Studies, as well as a minor in Public History. She earned her graduate degree in Interdisciplinary Studies from the University of Washington–Tacoma and is an award-winning Texas journalist.

She resides in Kenedy, Texas, and was a history columnist for the *Victoria Advocate*.